CHINA CRY

The Nora Lam Story

Nora Lam

with
Irene Burk Harrell

WORD BOOKS
PUBLISHER
WACO, TEXAS

CHINA CRY: THE NORA LAM STORY

Scripture Quotations are from The King James Version of the Bible

ISBN 0-8499-2898-2
Library of Congress Catalog Card Number: 79-63932
Printed in the United States of America

to my Chinese people
one-fourth of the world's population
who so desperately need to know Jesus

CONTENTS

FOREWORD

In *China Cry* you meet a remarkable woman and my good friend, Nora Lam Sung. You travel with her as she dramatically escapes from Mainland China, sharing each breathtaking experience on her journey to freedom. You live with her through her transition period in Hong Kong and her struggle to find a new life in America—not only a new life but a new ministry, to reach the Chinese people with the good news of Jesus Christ!

When in China last fall, I met a young woman who had never heard the name of Jesus! Many of the billion Chinese people on the Mainland and Taiwan have never heard of Jesus Christ. *China Cry* is their story too. They need to hear about their Savior!

It is my prayer that after reading *China Cry* you will join Nora, me, and others in praying for revival in China.

DEDE (MRS. PAT) ROBERTSON
June 1980

WRITER'S PREFACE

For me, it all began on a hot day in August, with a phone call from my friend, Floyd Thatcher, who is editorial director for Word Books in Waco, Texas. "Have you ever heard of Nora Lam?" he wanted to know.

"Nora Lam? Sounds familiar . . . Oh, yes! She's the Chinese evangelist, isn't she? The woman who was put in front of a firing squad, and they fired, but—" Shivers ran down my spine as I remembered.

"Nora needs someone to help her write a new book," Floyd said. "Would you be able to go to California to meet her, to see if you two could work together?"

A Texas publisher calling a North Carolina writer to do a book for a Chinese woman living in California? That *had* to be the Lord. Indeed I would like to meet the woman of many miracles. . . .

Meet her I did, on a beautiful September morning in San Jose, and less than two weeks later, after a number of amazing "coincidences" in my own life (*I* call them miracles), I was embarking on an unforgettable journey with Nora Lam Sung—to the other side of the world. As the giant 747 droned for endless hours across the vast

Pacific, Nora told me her life story. Her tears and mine splashed on the tape recorders and notebooks in our laps as she relived the incredible years for me. In the interviewing that followed, Nora and I didn't always understand one another. My questions came from a sheltered American mind, and Nora's answers came from a broken Chinese heart. Often, when we came to an impasse that words could not bridge, Nora would shrug her shoulders and remind me, "Irene, it's a whole different culture, a whole different culture."

What I experienced in Taiwan, in Hong Kong, in Macao impressed me that Nora was right about that—there were chopsticks instead of forks, bicycle-jammed streets, rice paddies alongside skyscrapers—so much that seemed strange and unreal. But always, everywhere we went, even in the midst of tears, Nora kept smiling and saying "God is *so* good!" And being with her, I began to see his goodness more clearly than ever before. To recount all the marvels we saw together as we worked on this book would take another book! But let me share one thing, because it has special significance to me:

One day while we were in Taiwan, Nora turned to me with an abrupt, "Irene, you must come back with me in July for the Crusade. You'll need to see that."

Well, she was right, but it was impossible for me to go. Our fourteen-year-old Marguerite would be home for the summer from her far-away school for the deaf, and I wouldn't want to leave her. "Bring her along!" Nora said, in the crisp voice I had heard before when she thought something was all settled. But a million difficulties ricocheted in my mind . . . Nora just didn't understand!

Of course she *did* understand—not God's plan, not human limitations—far better than I. Marguerite and I did go to the Crusade, and our mission-minded daughter, Alice, went too. The three of us shared the adventure of a lifetime as we got to know—and to love immensely—

Nora, her godly husband S. K. Sung, her seven beautiful children and two beautiful daughters-in-law. We became one family, their lives indelibly etched on ours.

One night on our way home from Taiwan, I sat praying in the huge ballroom of the Philippine Plaza Hotel, watching as an unending throng streamed to the platform so Nora could pray for them. Suddenly Nora shouted, "God has just told me that people are being healed of deafness in their left ear! Come to the platform and claim your healing!"

I wondered what to do. Marguerite had become tired from the long day, and Alice had gone with her to our room. Just then Nora said, "Where is the little girl with two hearing aids who came all the way from America?"

No longer wondering, I hurried to our room. Alice and I roused Marguerite, and the three of us made our way back into the ballroom. 'Guerite went up on the platform so Nora could lay hands on her and pray.

When 'Guerite came down, she looked at Alice and shook her head. "It didn't work," she said. But a few days later, 'Guerite started complaining that her left hearing aid was too loud. She kept using almost-dead batteries in it to tone it down. Something was happening.

When she went back to school in the fall, I was sure the audiograms would show dramatic improvement in the hearing in her left ear. They didn't—the official hearing test recorded the same hearing level it had for years. But a note on the audiogram said, "The maximum power output of one of 'Guerite's aids was too high, causing some sounds to be uncomfortably loud for her. We have adjusted the aid so it is now appropriate for her."

A few days ago, I telephoned 'Guerite at school. She had lots of news. "Mom, guess what! I'm going to graduate! And the audiologist told me that pretty soon I'm going to be wearing only one hearing aid!"

"Really? How come?"

"Well, when I put my left aid in my ear and turn up the volume, I hear just the same as I do without it."

What do these things mean? We ponder them in our hearts, whispering hallelujahs at miracles fifteen years in the making, knowing there is an "appointed time" for all things and believing with all our hearts that what God begins, he is able to finish to perfection. "If you can believe," Jesus said. "All things are possible to him that believes." Without faith, it doesn't happen. To an unbelieving generation, no sign is given, but to us who believe, the signs never end.

"According to your faith be it unto you." Faith is one of the ingredients God uses to make it happen, and He has given to every one of us the measure of faith we need. My prayer is that you will bring that measure of faith to your reading of Nora's story and become, with her, one of God's instruments for reaching the lost world with the Good News of Jesus.

Nora Lam Sung is a real woman of God, perhaps the most powerful woman in the world today, not because of who *she* is, but because He has chosen her for this great and glorious purpose, and she has said—and keeps on saying—"Yes, Lord."

Let us say it too.

Irene Burk Harrell
Wilson, North Carolina
Spring 1980

1

FIRING SQUAD

I was a young girl, only seventeen, in 1949 when the Communists took over my beloved country of China. They swept in like a Red tidal wave, toppling all the richness of centuries-old tradition before them, proclaiming bright hopes for the future to a land that was tired of war, sick of poverty—a fertile field for the glowing promises of anything new.

"We want everybody to be equal," the Communists said. "We don't want the landlords and bankers and professional people to be richer than anyone else. We want everybody to have enough to eat."

It sounded so good, I almost became one of them. I adopted the Communist look—short straight hair, no nylons, no jewelry, no make-up—and I wore the ubiquitous plain gray shirt and slacks. We all looked alike, and none of us smiled. It was easier to follow their way than to put oneself in an awkward situation by being different. That might not be comfortable—nor safe.

I was enrolled in Soochow University in Shanghai, studying to be a lawyer. One day I was sitting in a classroom hearing the same teaching I'd heard a million times before—how every form of animal life in the world came from a microscopic cell that gradually evolved into fish and birds and mammals. The professor said man had descended from monkeys by the evolutionary process.

Although I had swallowed this line of thinking many times in the past, that day a question arose in my mind.

"If monkeys became men," I asked the professor, "why don't they do it now? Why don't monkeys come down from the trees today and turn into human beings?"

The look on his face warned me I should never argue with Communist teaching again.

"Capitalists will try to enslave you with their religion!" he shouted. "They will die out because of overproduction! They will have to throw their excess cars into the ocean when no one can buy them!"

Yes, I remembered learning that, and for a time I put my questionings to rest. A few years later, it was plain that the intimidating brainwashing had had the desired effect on me. One cloudy afternoon when my husband Kai Sing and I were riding along a busy street in a pedicab, we passed a church that still had a cross on the top of it. The cross stood out against the gray sky and caught my attention.

"Do you still believe in Jesus, Kai Sing?" I asked him, since he had been a Christian once, just as I had been.

Then, before he could open his mouth to answer, I said, "I don't. There's no God. I don't believe anymore."

He didn't say a word. Like most of the people in those days, he was too confused to know what he thought. But I felt I had found the truth, that I was wiser than I had been when I believed in the Lord.

In 1953 I received my law degree, graduating as the third honor student from the top in a class of 375. Only twenty years old, going on twenty-one, I thought I was a genius. I held my head high, my nose in the air, as I marched up and received my diploma. The Communists must have thought I was a genius too. I was the only girl chosen from my class to be an assistant professor, teaching history and political science to Communist soldiers in a "speed school" at Tung Tsi, which had been a famous architectural school before the Communists took it over. There, six normal years of instruction were given in three years of concentrated teaching.

I was very proud of myself and my accomplishments. There were many benefits to cooperating with the Communists—prestige, esteem, ego satisfaction, the hope of a glorious future. What they promised was like a beautiful dream, and I was willing to make sacrifices to see the dream come true.

But suddenly the dream came to an end. We woke up to the reality of rumors we had tried not to hear—rumors of wholesale murder and destruction. Suddenly they came too close for us to deny them any longer. The bright promises we had embraced in our youthful idealism proved to be empty words, deceitfully spoken, with no hope or intention of fulfillment.

Every day landlords were shot without trial, and their property was seized. Their wives and children were subjected to brutal torture and merciless slaughter by the Communist soldiers. Pastors of churches were taken away in the middle of the night and never heard from again. Bibles were picked up and burned. Intellectuals were stripped of their positions and sent to labor camps to load coal or feed hogs.

Constant brainwashing was the order of the new day. The object seemed to be to make everyone a meaningless, mindless part of a huge machine—without individuality, without personal purpose, without beauty or freedom. Without hope. And spies were everywhere. Nobody dared to be honest with anybody else for fear "they" would find out. Even husbands and wives refrained from expressing their real feelings to one another, because the Communists might be listening.

Overnight, the suicide rate soared. People jumped from

rooftops, cut their wrists and drained their lifeblood in their bathrooms, or hung themselves in their backyards because of the intolerable persecution at the hands of the Communists. My husband was being persecuted at the court where he worked, my father at the hospital where he practiced medicine. And in 1955, real persecution began for school and college professors who had been servants of the State. It began happening to people I knew! Every day we heard shots outside the school and saw soldiers passing by the windows. We were afraid even to look at one another. The father of one of my girlfriends was put to death for expressing disagreement with the regime. Every night I heard trucks coming to pick up dead bodies.

And all at once, the persecution was happening to me.

It was a hot humid morning in the summer of 1955. I had spent the night in the school dormitory, as I did sometimes instead of taking the long, late ride home. Awakening early, vomiting with the distressing morning sickness of my first pregnancy, I washed my face and put on my drab "uniform" for the seven o'clock meeting which was the first order of the day for all the teachers.

The whole staff was required to attend. There was usually news of some kind from Peking, the Communist capital of Mainland China. And then we had to hear something read from Chairman Mao's Little Red Book of sayings, which was supposed to have an answer for everything.

There was a guard outside the auditorium door, as there had been so often lately, and I had discovered the outside doors of the school were locked, keeping the five thousand students and faculty members virtual prisoners. For several days, one member or another of the staff had been questioned in the morning meeting, the Communists taking down their answers and requiring them to put their thumbprints on the papers afterward.

That morning, about fifty people were herded into the

large meeting room. Some of them were Communists, some were fellow teachers. We were seated in a large circle, each person facing the others, and all at once the Communist in charge of the meeting was looking straight at me.

"I want to ask you some questions," he barked in a no-nonsense tone of voice. I felt my heart beat faster. They were after me! But what had I done? Too late, and with a sudden sinking feeling, I realized that a girl I knew, in whose home I had visited, was always telling me the "good things" about Communism. Because I had considered her to be my friend, I had confided to her some things about my family background. It was a terrible mistake—she was one of "them"—but it was too late to undo the damage now.

I had seen other professors weep, get sick, or faint when it was their turn to be questioned, but I was determined to be strong.

The faces of the other teachers in the big circle showed relief that *they* weren't being called on the carpet. The relief was mingled with fear, however, because they knew their day would inevitably arrive.

Questions came from everywhere at once, as hard and fast as machine-gun fire and meant to be as deadly:

"How did your grandfather become so rich?—Why did he own almost the whole bank of China?—Why was your mother so kind to the American missionaries?—Why did she and your father always visit the concentration camps during the Japanese war and wash the feet of the American soldiers?—Why did they take sweaters to them, and food, medicine, and bandages?—Why did your father go to France for his education?—Why did you marry a man from Hong Kong instead of a Communist?—Tell us the names of all your professors.—How did they feel about Christianity?—What do you know about the underground church?—Why did Professor Ling kill himself?—Who is hiding Bibles in the dormitory? . . ."

The questions went on and on relentlessly, and I knew I had come to the end of the road. Some people who'd been questioned so hostilely had simply disappeared from school. No one knew where they had gone—or been taken. A few had thought they could save their own lives by betraying someone else, but it never worked. I knew that if I gave them the answers they wanted, I'd be killed anyway.

When I paused before answering the questions, the Communists slapped my face until it was red with stinging. When I answered with just a word or two, trying not to get anyone else in trouble, they kicked my shins with their canvas boots and shouted at me. When I didn't know an answer, they shoved me and screamed the questions even louder. Before the morning was over, I felt like a thousand people were screaming at me at the same time.

When the Communists wore themselves out, a new group of questioners came in and took their place. The barrage of insinuating questions never slowed.

By the middle of the afternoon, I was aware of being terribly thirsty, but there was no water for me. Then, from somewhere in the deep recesses of my mind, soothing, resonant, inviting words rose to my consciousness:

"Come to Me and drink, and I will give you rivers of living water. You will never thirst again."

I was hungry, but there was no food. Again, familiar words rose up inside me without my volition:

"Man shall not live by bread alone. I am the Bread of Life."

I was tired, but there was no one to take my place, no way for me to rest. Once more, refreshing, reassuring words were spoken:

"Come unto Me, all you who labor and are heavy laden, and I will give you rest."

I recognized the source of the words. They were from the Holy Bible, God's Word. Strangely, they comforted me and made me ready for the next question. It was louder and angrier than any of the others, as if my interrogators had gathered all their fury and compacted it into one awful, capital, condemnation:

"Are you a Christian?—Are you a Christian?—ARE YOU A CHRISTIAN?"

Someone had taken my chair, and I was standing in the midst of them. They crowded around, spitting the question at me, cursing me, tearing my clothes.

Only half-conscious of their fury, I asked myself the question:

"Am I a Christian? Am I a Christian?"

For a moment, time stopped. My accusers faded into invisibility. Their raucous voices were beyond my hearing as I looked at—and listened to—memories stored inside me, things I had buried in my subconscious along with my questions about evolution . . .

I was remembering the day I had run eagerly to an altar and invited Jesus into my heart. I was hearing again the songs the American missionaries had taught me when I was a young schoolgirl. I was recalling the times when God had sent an angel to comfort me.

Yes! God *was* real—more real than anything that was happening around me. Jesus had *died* for me, but if I would not confess Him before men, He would not confess me before His Father—and my Father—in heaven.

My mind must have been asleep under all the brainwashing, all the fear, but now it was alive to the Truth again. I knew I had to choose whether I wanted to belong to the Lord or belong to the devil for eternity.

It was not a hard decision for me to make.

"O Lord," I cried, "forgive me! Forgive me for everything! Lord, let me be Your child again!"

The ugly pride, the self-centeredness and conceit, the

unbelief and neglect of His Word, the disobedience and failure to seek His will—I could feel all of them leaving me in a great flood of cleansing. And the peace of God came down from heaven like a river. I knew that I belonged to the King of kings and the Lord of lords again.

"Stand up, stand up for Jesus, ye soldiers of the cross . . ."

The challenging words of the old hymn filled my mind and heart, and I wanted to act upon them. If I would ever stand up for Jesus, it had to be now. With a surge of strength that had to be His strength made perfect in my weakness, I was ready to answer the question being screamed at me by my enemies, their faces contorted with rage, their eyes bulging with hate:

"ARE YOU A CHRISTIAN? ARE YOU A—"

"Yes," I answered strongly, clearly. "I was not a good Christian in the past, but I surely want to be one now. I'm not going to deny Jesus, no matter what you do to me."

They saw that I meant it, and furthermore that I would not betray my family or my friends, even if they questioned me from then until the end of the world.

"TAKE HER OUT AND KILL HER!"

It was six o'clock in the evening. My eyes were bruised, my mouth and nose were bleeding. My clothes were ripped, and my back was aching where they had hit me and hit me and hit me. But what peace I had!

I followed the Communists from the room, down the hallway, out onto the gravel road that hurt my feet through the thin soles of my worn-out shoes. We seemed to walk forever. Several times I tripped and fell. Those nearest to me jerked me up by my arms, digging their fingernails into the soft flesh. Finally we came to a field where several bodies were lying motionless, face down as if they had fallen. The Communists stopped near the bodies, so I stopped too.

Close by, I could see a red truck with a machine gun

and a spotlight mounted on top of it. Several vultures circled ominously in an unclouded sky. When I spotted seven or eight uniformed soldiers with rifles on their shoulders, I knew they were a firing squad. And I knew it was my time to die.

One of the Communists jerked a cord from his pocket and roughly tied my hands behind my back. Another knotted a foul-smelling rag across my eyes and around my head as a blindfold, cursing as he did it. The third one asked, sneeringly, if I had any message I wanted to leave for my mother. He said he would write a note for me.

I knew that if I told him anything to write, he would use it to persecute my family, so I said nothing. But I thought about my mother, and how much I loved her. Who would tell her I was dead? I knew she would cry, and I wondered if she would be allowed to claim my body and bury it. Or would the vultures—?

I wouldn't think about that. Or about the baby inside me who would never be born . . .

"You have three minutes to live!" the shout came, and then, insinuatingly, trying to tempt me, "You are such a young, intelligent girl. You don't need to die. If you will only deny your God, we can let you go."

But I had made my decision.

"I want You, Jesus," I said in my heart. "I'm never going to deny You. Live or die, I'm Yours."

I had given up completely. His will be done. And then something inside me insisted that I speak to Him out loud, lifting up His name so "they" would have to hear it:

"Lord Jesus, give me a chance to live, that I may serve You. Lord Jesus, give my baby a chance to live."

The three minutes were up. Bolts clicked as bullets slid into their chambers. Then came the shout:

"One, two, three, FIRE!"

I heard the crack of rifles. I tensed for the impact of bullets ripping through my flesh. And I fell to the ground.

2

BEGINNINGS

How had I come to such a tragic place?

Let me tell you my life story . . .

My earliest memories are of a childhood spent as a pampered, spoiled little rich girl, an only child in the family of a well-to-do doctor in Shanghai. My mother bought me the most expensive clothes from Europe and America. I was always dressed like Shirley Temple, the blonde, curly-haired child actress of Hollywood, and I had a Shirley Temple doll dressed exactly like me. Almost every week, my picture was on the society page of the *China Post*, modeling one of my new outfits from America.

Because I was flatfooted, my father had special shoes made to order for me so I wouldn't suffer. Everything possible was done for my pleasure, comfort, and safety.

A governess was with me constantly during the day, and a nurse or maid hovered over me at night. I never played in the yard, walked the dog, or did anything else without the governess, the gardener, the chauffeur, maid, nurse, or private tutor following me. But I didn't see my parents often. My father was busy with his medical practice during the day; my mother led the expected life of a rich "society" woman. In the evening, both of them were constantly going to parties or giving parties of their own.

One day when I was four or five years old, I decided I wanted to play by myself for a while, so I fled from my governess down the elegantly carpeted staircase of our beautiful home. As I ran, my little feet stumbled on the thick red carpet, and I fell headlong to the bottom of the stairs. The governess's face was ashen when she reached my side and picked me up in her arms. And she almost fainted when she saw a little cut in the middle of my forehead.

Panic overtook all the servants. The princess was injured! What could they do? The cook, who had more presence of mind—if less wisdom—than the rest of them, took a handful of fish bone meal and rubbed it into the wound to stop the bleeding. How I reveled in all the attention!

When my father got home, he rushed me to the hospital. But it was too late to properly cleanse the wound, and I was to bear a little scar forever.

My father was so upset over my accident that he scolded everyone on the household staff, from the chief maid down to the chauffeur. All were punished because the dear little princess was hurt. The unfortunate episode had been all my fault, and I knew it. But I never offered to take the blame.

Whenever I wanted something, I got it. My mother often told me she would get me the moon if I wanted it and she could reach that high. I never wanted the moon, but I was determined to have my own way about whatever I did want.

One day a maid threw away one of my treasures—an old, dirty, square-faced green cloth dog. When I found out about it, I stomped my little foot and screamed at the top of my lungs.

"Make a new one for me right now! Exactly like the old one! Or I won't go to bed tonight!"

"Yes, dear," she said, afraid someone would hear me

and she would be punished for my outburst. "I'll make you a new one right away."

She found some scraps of material in the sewing basket and started cutting out a new dog for me that very moment. When she had finished it, I snatched it from her hands and went to sleep with the dog in my arms. No princess in a royal palace ever got her own way more than I did.

But my days as a princess having her own way came abruptly to an end when I was seven years old. Japanese invaders took over our country and our beautiful estate, giving us just a few hours to get out or be killed. We knew they had no mercy, so we fled for our lives, taking only what we could carry in our hands. I took my Shirley Temple doll, of course, but left most of my clothes behind. The Japanese kept all our rings, watches, diamonds, money—everything of value. Overnight, we became penniless.

There was only one place for us to go, and that was to the house of my father's stepmother. I dreaded it, because I knew she had been cruel to him when he was a boy. To escape her tyranny, he had gone to school in France at the age of thirteen and stayed until he had graduated from the University of Lyon as a medical doctor. He still suffered from asthma and bronchitis because when he was young she had never permitted him to have enough clothing to keep warm during the cold winter months.

My grandmother's house was something to behold—big, gray, and, to me, incredibly ugly, just like everything inside it. Grandmother lived with her two daughters and their children in the new part of the house. My father, mother, and I were given one room with a bath on the second floor of an old three-story wing that hadn't been lived in for years. There was very little furniture in our room, just a bed and dresser for my parents and a box for me to sleep on, with a chair placed at the end of it for my legs and feet. The other rooms were closed off, and scary, dust-laden spiderwebs were everywhere.

The entire first floor of the old wing was used for hanging and drying salted meat that would later be cooked and offered as sacrifices before idols. Watching over the meat, so no one would dare to steal a scrap of it, were grandmother's hideous Buddhas glaring out of every corner. How I hated the sightless glass eyes of those lifeless gods of stone and clay! And the shadowy chunks of meat looked like so many devils waving back and forth above me, threatening to fall and crush me beneath them. The house was a devil's house—a terrifying place for a "princess" like me.

Every day grandmother would ask the Buddhas if anyone had stolen anything. She was always accusing one of her many servants of wrongdoing, and she yelled at them from morning until night.

Grandmother had strange eating habits that were also connected with her worship of Buddha. She never left the tiniest scrap of food on her plate, but always cleaned every dish, because Buddha had told her that for every clean plate she could buy one more acre of land.

I wasn't used to the foolish superstitions of a Buddha-centered life, and I could feel evil all over the house. Wherever I went, Buddhas stared at me with their lifeless eyes—large Buddhas and small ones—along with the goddess of mercy and other idols. They kept me in a nightmare of fear, but nothing could be done about it. We had to live somewhere.

Grandmother not only worshiped idols, she also worshiped her ancestors. On every ancestor's birthday and death day, special dishes were cooked and offered on the table where incense was burning in front of the picture of the departed ancestor. Everyone was supposed to kneel before the sacrifice to honor the ancestor, and then they could eat the special food.

Since my parents and I had no kitchen, and they were usually gone at mealtimes, I had to eat with grandmother and her family. They always scolded me at the dinner table and let me eat only the leftovers and scraps they didn't want for themselves.

Grandmother seemed to harbor an intense hatred of me, and she delighted in forcing me to eat the awful, greasy skin of the duck's neck. She would put it on my plate with her chopsticks and then threaten me in front of everyone:

"I warn you! If you don't eat it, I will have Buddha jab at you with his chopsticks and pull your hair out piece by piece."

Scared to death, I would try to choke the skin down while tears streamed down my cheeks. But my throat refused to swallow the awful food. Sometimes I couldn't stop gagging and retching and would have to flee from the table in embarrassment, with all of them laughing at me. I often went to bed hungry, but I didn't tell my parents, because I didn't want to hurt their feelings or worry them. No longer like a darling princess in a royal palace, I began to feel like a prisoner in an awful jail. The pampered little rich girl was growing up fast. And it was hard.

In spite of the war and my father's medical practice, my parents continued to have an active social life, and were often out late at night playing mahjong, a popular gambling game, with their friends. I had gone overnight from living a life in which someone was with me every moment night and day to one in which I was alone most of the time. I spent many hours crying with loneliness and fear in the frightening old wing of grandmother's house.

Sometimes at night, I would sneak over to the maid's room above the garage and crawl into bed with her until my parents came home. When they knocked on the garage door for the maid to unlock the huge wrought-iron gate in the courtyard, I'd whisper, "Wait! Let me run back first."

And while the maid put on her robe to go down and let my parents in, I'd roll out of her warm bed and race down the stairs at the back of the garage, tear across the courtyard with the fishpond reflecting eerie shadows, and sneak into the frightening old house past the smelly, cobwebby hanging devils that grabbed for me. Then I'd climb up the dark, creaking stairway and into my cold bed, my heart pounding out of me. There I'd try to stop shivering while I pretended to be asleep.

Sometimes when my parents were out, I'd huddle on my makeshift bed and cry myself to sleep. If the telephone rang in the long dark hallway outside our room, I'd let it ring and ring. Then, shaking with fright, I would finally rush out to answer it—only to have the caller hang up as soon as I lifted the receiver. Then I'd go back to bed to cry myself to sleep again.

Soon after we moved to my grandmother's house, I began to go to elementary school at the McTyier Christian School. For the first time in my life, I heard about Jesus, called the Son of God, who was living in the world today although no one could see Him. *How could this be?* I wondered. It was a mystery too big for my child's mind to grasp.

But I enjoyed singing the hymns and hearing the missionaries tell stories of Jesus and His love for the children. I was also told that He wanted to be my friend. That seemed so wonderful to me that sometimes, when I was lonely and frightened, I would pretend to talk to my invisible friend, Jesus. It seemed to help a little. But I needed a friend I could see.

In my dreadful unhappiness, I often wondered why my grandmother and her family mistreated me so. And I wondered what my cousins meant when they taunted me and called me a "wild seed from hell." I didn't understand it; I only knew it sounded ugly, and it hurt me terribly. For a while I could forget about all that when I was at school, but before long one of my cousins spread the word there that I was a "wild seed," and my former school friends began to call me names and insult me too. They said my mother and father were not my real parents at all, but that I was an unwanted child who had been abandoned in a hospital. Then school became a nightmare of loneliness too.

I couldn't stand it any longer, so one day I summoned the courage to ask my mother what it was all about.

"People keep calling me dirty names," I told her. "They say that I came from somewhere else and that you're not my real mother. Please tell me the truth about it, and I promise I'll never ask you again."

Mother looked very thoughtful for a long minute, making up her mind about something. Then she patted the bed and said, "Sit down, child, and I will tell you all about yourself. It's time for you to know."

I perched on the edge of the bed while she sat down in the chair and started to talk. I listened, enchanted, unable to speak, while the story unfolded. It sounded like a sad but beautiful fairy tale—only it was true.

"You were born—and abandoned—in the Wee Yo Hospital, an old missionary hospital, in Peking in 1932," mother began. "Your mother was a teenager, in love with a handsome opera star. She came from a high, famous family, was well-educated and very beautiful. Your real father was very much in love with her, highly educated himself, and very handsome. But in China one must marry within the class into which he is born, and your real mother was more highborn than he. Her parents would not give their consent to the marriage, despite your father's talent, and so your mother had no choice but to abandon you in the hospital. I'm sure it broke her heart to leave her precious baby with strangers."

I could feel tears forming in the corners of my eyes at the thought of a young mother having to leave her baby.

"My cousin, Dr. Soo," mother went on, "happened to be an intern in the hospital when you were born. She was studying to be a baby doctor. She knew your father and I had been married for many years and that we had been unable to have any children of our own. Since you were such a cute baby, she thought we might like to have you, so she wrote us a letter and sent us your picture. Meanwhile, instead of turning you over to a state orphanage, she kept you in the hospital until she heard from us."

I was holding my breath, hoping my mother would take me.

"The minute I saw your beautiful baby picture, I knew you were meant for me. Your father knew it too. We got in touch with Dr. Soo right away and asked her to hire a nanny for you until you were old enough to travel. When you were just six months old, your nanny brought you to our house to live forever."

When mother had finished the story, she showed me a beautiful little black silk evening purse with an opal in the center of one side, surrounded by a cluster of tiny diamonds. Opening the clasp, she pulled out two little pictures of me, taken when I was only a week old. There was also a paper with a lot of writing on it, giving all the details of my birth and adoption.

For a moment, seeing my pictures in the valuable little purse made me feel loved—and important.

"Oh, mother," I cried, "I'm so glad you adopted me! I will try to behave the rest of my life and become a nice person so other people will respect both of us."

Now I understood a little about why my cousins

persecuted me. Because I wasn't a blood relative, they felt I wasn't really a part of the family. To them, blood relationship was the most important thing. But already, from the teaching I was getting at the missionary school, and from the love my adoptive parents and I had for each other, I knew that love was far more important than blood. In fact, love was the most important thing of all.

But that knowledge didn't keep me from being lonely when my parents were away, and when my cousins kept making fun of me and refusing to let me take part in their celebrations. I might have died of loneliness at that time of my life if God hadn't sent the old man.

3

THE OLD MAN

My memories of the Japanese occupation of Shanghai blur into an unbelievable nightmare of indescribable terror. Every afternoon, like a frightened animal, I would run all the way home from school, past the rotting bodies hanging from the trees, past the Japanese soldiers whipping old ricksha men into the dust—bayoneting them if they cried out in protest. Past starving Chinese queued up in shoving, shivering, fearful lines to get their meager rice ration for the day, past the shoutings and screamings and sudden terrible silences of an occupied city.

When I finally reached the courtyard of my grandmother's house, I would pound on the front door, crying for someone to let me in, hammering at the door until my little fists were red with pain. Eventually grandmother or one of my taunting cousins would peer at me through the window, make a wicked face at me, and yell at me to come to the back door. When I stumbled around to the back, almost crazy with fear that the soldiers would get me, they'd send me back to the front again. Back and forth, back and forth, running from one door to the other. The "game" seemed to go on forever. My cousins would be cackling with fiendish glee on the inside while I was quaking with fear on the outside.

Eventually, someone would let me in, and I'd flee to the shadowy old wing, past the unchanging stares of the hideous Buddhas, up the scary cobwebby stairway, and into our lonely room to spend the interminable hours until my mother or father came in for the night. I was so heartbreakingly lonely that sometimes I would go into the bathroom and bury my face in the folds of mother's fleecy red bathrobe hanging on the back of the door and pretend she was in it—while I sobbed my heart out.

"God, help me! God, help me!" I cried one day. I knew that the stone Buddhas were powerless to help anyone, but maybe the God the missionaries talked about at my school could do something.

One afternoon as I was hugging my Shirley Temple doll, waiting for the hours to pass, crying because my cousins were having a party and I was not invited, I sensed that someone was in the room with me.

Opening my eyes, I saw an old Chinese man standing just inside the closed door. He was smiling at me, and he looked older than anyone I had ever seen before. His kindly face was full of wrinkles, and the hair of his head and beard was very long and very white. He was wearing the clothing of a servant, a long blue overshirt that hung to the floor.

How did he get in? I wondered. The door had been closed, and I hadn't heard any sound of it opening, nor of anyone coming up the stairs. He was just suddenly there. Dismissing his mysterious appearance from my mind, I told myself, "He's probably just one of grandmother's new servants."

Then he spoke softly, in the Mandarin dialect:

"Don't be afraid," he said. "I come from God." With that, he pointed a long bony finger upward. And then, as if he had been reading my mind, he continued, "You don't need to cry because you weren't invited to your cousins' party."

How did he know why I was crying?

"But I'm so lonely," I told him. "I don't have anyone to talk to—except Shirley, and she's only a doll."

"Sung Neng Yee," he said, calling me by my full Chinese name, "you have prayed to God, and He has heard your prayer. He has sent me to be your friend, to comfort you and help you."

"Shirley! Shirley!" I cried, hugging her close to me. "Did you hear that? The new God is real, and He has heard my prayer and sent us a friend!"

I was overjoyed to have someone to talk to—but what if he went away and never came back?

"Promise you'll come whenever I call you," I begged him.

He promised.

The next day, I told my mother about my new friend. She wanted me to call him right away so she could meet him, but I sensed he wouldn't come except when Shirley and I were alone.

Although I was the only one who ever saw him, the old man was helpful to us all. He came to see me almost every afternoon, and he would tell me such useful things as the best time to get in line for the rice ration for our family. And one day, the old man brought wonderful news:

"You are going to escape from Shanghai and this house full of Buddhas," he said. "It will be a long, hard journey, but you will escape to a faraway city and meet your grandfather."

I knew grandfather was in Chungking, where he'd been when the war began, and that Chungking was the wartime capital of our country. It had never been captured by the Japanese. But how would we be able to go there? The Japanese would never allow us to escape. Still, the old man had said it would come to pass, and I knew I could always depend on his word.

I was so happy to think of leaving my grandmother's

house that I laughed and cried at the same time. When I told my mother and father the news, they could hardly believe it. To be in Chungking would be to live in freedom, they said.

"Call the old man back and ask him all the details," mother begged.

I told her she would have to leave the room first, so she did. Then I prayed and asked God to send the old man to see me again. In a few moments, he was standing inside the door in the same place where he usually appeared.

"Please, my friend," I said, "my mother and father want to know all the details—exactly when and how we are going to get away from Shanghai."

"Tell them that in about one week, they will hear a knock on their door. A messenger will come and tell them exactly what to do."

As quickly as he had come, he had vanished again, and my parents came back to hear the news.

Sure enough, a week later, there was a knock at the front door. We opened it to admit a man we had never seen before. He identified himself only as a secret agent sent by my grandfather. Then he spoke to my father:

"Your father has sent me to bring you and your family to Chungking," he said. "The trip will be about fifteen hundred miles long. Our transportation will be uncertain, and we will have to walk some of the way, crossing through forests and climbing mountains because we will have to hide from the Japanese soldiers. We will have many weeks of travel before we can even think of crossing into free China."

That much sounded exciting, but then he warned us, "It will be dangerous, and perhaps some of you may even die on the way. But those who make it will be able to live in freedom once again—with plenty of food to eat."

I was so happy the old man's words were coming true that I had to tell Shirley.

"Shirley, the trip will be hard," I said, "but we will make it because the old man told me so."

"I'm sorry," the secret agent said, shaking his head sternly when he saw the doll in my arms. "The child will have to leave her doll behind. A beggar would not have such a doll, and you must all go as beggars so no one will suspect you are escaping to Chungking."

Forced to leave Shirley behind with one of the cousins who had been so hateful to me, I couldn't keep from crying. And when I saw the dirty, ragged clothes that were prepared for me to wear, and was told I had to smear dirt on my face to complete the disguise, I asked my mother, "Do I really have to wear those awful rags?"

"Yes," she said, dressing in rags herself and disheveling her hair. "It will be a small price to pay for freedom."

I didn't understand much about freedom, but I knew that no price was too great to pay to escape my grandmother and her Buddhas.

The train station where our escape was to begin was so noisy with confusion and so crowded with people that I soon forgot the rags I was wearing and the dirt smeared on my face. I could only stand and stare at the hundreds of bodies pushing and shoving about me, their eyes never noticing the eleven-year-old girl in their midst.

Leaving Shanghai was hard for my mother. She would miss her friends and the endless round of mahjong parties. My father was angry at leaving all his property to the Japanese. But getting away from grandmother and the hideous Buddhas was wonderful to me. Besides, I would enjoy being with my parents for a change, no matter where we went. Even the crush of the bodies of strangers about me was welcome at first. They were people, real flesh-and-blood human beings.

But after a few moments, when the train chugged into the station and opened its doors for more passengers, the bodies surrounding me didn't act human. They were more like crazed animals, pushing, clawing, screaming, trying to get a place on the train. I didn't mind being jostled along with the crowd until all at once I felt suddenly alone in the midst of them. Fear clutched my heart as I turned my head frantically in all directions. My parents were nowhere to be seen!

I panicked, darting between people, pushing and shoving, trying in vain to see over the crowd of hundreds of milling people.

"God, help me!" I cried. "Don't let them leave without me! God, please help me!"

Suddenly there they were, standing on the edge of the crowd, looking for me.

"Mother! Mother!" I screamed. "Don't leave me! Here I am!" I ran to her and clung to her long beggar's dress with the thick quilted padding inside. Sobbing with relief, I thanked God that He had heard and answered my prayer, that He was really alive, not like Buddhas made of stone and clay.

The three of us jammed our way onto the crowded train. The seats and aisles were so full, the people packed so close together, that it was impossible for anyone to fall down when we lurched out of the station.

I clutched my mother's hand tightly, fearing I would be lost from her again. Slowly the miles went by. The train became much too hot, with the overpowering stench of humanity scared and packed too tightly together. Some of the women fainted, but there was no place to lay them down. Their limp bodies had to be held upright between their friends. I watched in fascination as their heads wagged back and forth with the movement of the train, their faces expressionless white masks.

The trip to Nanking took eight hours. There was no food, no water, no means of sanitation, no opportunity to move around. The rags I was wearing chafed my skin and became slick with sweat. Every once in a while I would feel faint, and the world would begin closing with blackness to the size of a train tunnel. But still I was glad. With every mile, I was further from my grandmother, the lonely room, and the empty, staring Buddha eyes.

Finally the train slowed to a stop at Nanking.

"Oh, no! Not here too!" I heard the protest from my parents' lips.

"What is it?" I asked, and when they didn't answer, I wiggled my way to a window. There were the hated, sadistic Japanese soldiers outside, dressed in the uniform I feared, their faces full of evil.

Before we could leave the train, the soldiers opened every bag and parcel, strewing the contents on the ground outside, confiscating watches, rings, pens, flash-lights—everything of value. Because my parents and I looked like beggars and had the possessions of beggars, they let us go.

As we walked away from the station, I heard blood-curdling screams and turned to look back. The soldiers were pulling some of the younger, more attractive women out of the crowd. I wondered where they were taking them, and why. One young woman was clutching fran-tically at a man I supposed to be her husband, trying in vain to hold onto him. A soldier grabbed her fiercely and forced her to her knees. Then he jerked his bayonet from his side, and with one vicious chop cut off her head. The body fell limp, toppling into a pool of its own blood.

Another soldier grabbed a pretty young woman carry-ing a tiny baby. Terrified, she hugged the baby closer to her. With a demonic grin, the soldier wrenched the baby from her arms, tossed it up in the air, caught it on the tip of his bayonet, and slung the lifeless body into the crowd.

The horror of it all held me. I couldn't move, but then my father's hand mercifully turned me around to face in the other direction.

"Walk," he whispered. "Walk, and don't look back."

Eight hours after our arrival in Nanking, we gathered on the outskirts of the city with twenty-four other people who would be going with us to make the break for freedom. During the days we hid in bushes and behind trees, sleeping when we could. At night we walked or ran, keeping careful lookout for Japanese soldiers.

My shoes were soon worn out from stumbling over rugged paths and mountain trails, my feet sore and bleeding. Then mother took an old shirt and wrapped it around my feet for shoes. How good that felt!

Our food consisted chiefly of black buns and whatever we could buy along the way with the small amount of money that had escaped the eyes of the Japanese soldiers. Most of us came down with severe cases of dysentery. We lost weight and became too weak to carry even the small bundles of possessions we had brought along with us. Item after item was dropped along the way to lighten our loads.

Trudging over mountains, through deep valleys, along level plains, we all had sore hands and feet, and our aching bodies were bleeding from scratches and open wounds. Our faces were badly burned by the sun, our clothes hung in shreds, and yet we had to continue to press on. If we stopped, the others would be forced to leave us or die. We had all agreed to that at the beginning of the trip. In wartime China, paradoxically, life was so dear, it was also cheap.

None of us had realized how long and arduous our journey would be. But the hope of freedom kept us going.

Every night I would cry out to the living God. I seemed to be the only one who thought He would help us.

One day our flight to freedom almost came to an abrupt end. Bone-weary, we had stopped in a little shack along an overgrown path, where we huddled gratefully inside two small rooms and fell sound asleep. But not for long. Suddenly there was a loud crash as the doors were broken down.

Chinese bandits!

"Give us your money!" they shouted. We handed over everything we had left. Some of the bandits had been smoking opium, and it was obvious that they were half-crazed for more. They looked with lecherous eyes on the females in our group, but all must have been too ragged and filthy for their taste, so they walked away.

As soon as the bandits were out of sight, we fled for our lives, knowing they would turn us in to the nearest Japanese for a reward. We understood that we were about ten miles from the border, but we were so tired that even such a short distance seemed like halfway around the world. Would we ever make it?

We pushed on, and after hours of making ourselves put one foot in front of another we saw that we were approaching the border—a clearing about a mile wide. Our spirits fell to the depths when we saw too many Japanese soldiers guarding it, pacing up and down. We had come so far, but now our chances of escape to a free land looked hopeless. We could never hope to get by those guards with their sharp eyes. And we were too exhausted to turn back.

Many in the group—including my parents—felt that death was a certainty. We had spent thirty-seven days of living hell walking and running, suffering hunger and thirst—all for nothing.

Everyone around me began to wash their faces, hands, and feet, and to change their clothing. In a few hours, we would make the attempt to cross the border, and since they expected to be killed in the attempt, they wanted their bodies to be clean so their god would receive them. Our water supply was limited, and many people had to wash in the same water. The last one in line was going to be washing in mire.

Many people sat down to write notes to their relatives to tell them what to do with the possessions they had left behind. I wondered why they did that—how they expected their letters to be delivered when they were gone.

As I sat waiting for the time when we would attempt to cross the border, my mother came and gave me a ceremonial washing to prepare me for death. After she had finished, I was left alone again, and I knew I should pray.

"Living God, can You hear me? I hope so, because right now we need the help of a God who is real. Please help us cross the border. Make it so the Japanese soldiers don't see us. Amen."

As the blackness of night settled on the clearing, our guide whispered, "Now is the time." Hardly daring to breathe, we got up and started walking quietly toward the border. As we got nearer to it, we got down on our hands and knees and crawled over the last stretch until we could see freedom just ahead. With all the strength left in us, we stood up and charged over the last few yards.

For some strange reason, the Japanese never saw us or heard us. Could God have heard my prayer and blinded their eyes and stopped their ears?

"Freedom!" we shouted, safe in the province of Szechwan, knowing we had made it against all the odds.

The land of freedom was a barren desert, but we fell gratefully onto the parched dry ground and watered it with our tears as we sang our national anthem.

4

CHUNGKING

Yes, we were in a free province, but we were still a long way from Chungking, the capital of China, where my grandfather lived. There was still great hardship ahead, miles of walking through snow-covered mountains with frostbitten hands and feet so painful we thought we couldn't go another step. When we were all ready to give up, we spotted a truck that had been left behind by the Japanese. It was a strange-looking vehicle that burned charcoal instead of gasoline, and was propelled by a steam engine. I'd never seen anything like it before. We all gathered wood and were soon on our way with wheels under us!

The winding road through the mountains was very narrow. At times, we had to get out of the truck because the wheels were only inches from the edge of steep cliffs and we feared we would plunge to our deaths on the rocks below. We could see where other trucks and buses had fallen over, probably carrying hundreds of people to painful death in the valley. After all we had endured already, we didn't want our journey to end like that.

As we approached the city of Chungking in our strange vehicle, all twenty-seven of us were still alive. How grateful we were!

We arrived in Chungking just after the New Year. People were streaming into the city from all directions to escape the horrors of the Japanese occupation.

When we arrived within sight of my grandfather's house, I could hardly believe my eyes. It was perched at the very top of a hill all its own, and there were five flights of steep stairs leading to it. We were all really puffing when we reached the top. It was noontime, and my grandfather was not at home, but we were greeted by the wife of my father's half-brother and her children, one a girl about my age. I went to the kitchen for some welcome food, and then to the room where I could unpack my beggar's clothes.

When grandfather, the chairman of the board of the Bank of China, arrived at five o'clock, and I was introduced to him for the first time, I just stood and stared. I had heard so much about him all my life, and there he was, the most interesting-looking man I had ever seen. His eyes looked just as little and piercing as I had heard they did. He seemed to be wearing a very old suit, with several layers of heavy underclothing beneath it. He walked with a stick. But more remarkable than anything else about him were his ears—they hung down almost as long as the side of his head, and there was a cord leading from one of them to a hearing aid in his pocket. I knew it wasn't polite, but I couldn't help staring.

Grandfather was looking me over too. Then he asked brusquely, "Child, don't you have any decent clothes to wear?"

Strangely, I wasn't afraid of him; I detected a note of friendliness under his gruff exterior.

My father explained for me that we had been forced to travel as beggars and leave our clothing behind. He gave a little snort of approval—or disapproval, I couldn't tell which—and asked another granddaughter, who was about my size, if she didn't have something she could give me in place of the rags I was wearing. Mother got a dress from her sister-in-law, and father put on one of his father's suits, so the matter of suitable clothing was soon taken care of.

I could tell that grandfather's family was very rich and cultured. There was a lot of beautiful, very expensive furniture in the house, but it was a very different home from the ones to which I had been accustomed in Shanghai. To begin with, Chungking was not as modern a city as Shanghai, and there was no electricity or running water in the house. All water had to be carried in from the outside. I soon learned to be very conservative, using every pitcher or basinful for several purposes before it was thrown out.

Coping with the water situation every day was quite a chore. We had to carry most of it up from the Yangtze River, and it was always full of mud. We sprinkled alum in it so the mud would sink to the bottom and we could dip relatively clear water from the top. Many people were accustomed to washing their clothes and taking their baths in the river, and it seemed strange to me that we had to drink the same water.

Taking a bath in grandfather's house was a delightful experience for me. I would drag a large wooden tub into the warm kitchen and sit in it cross-legged like a Buddha to wash myself. About halfway through with my bath, the wood would become soaked, and water would start leaking out onto the bare wood floor. Then I would race to see if I could get the soap rinsed off before the water was all gone. Instead of presenting an inconvenience, taking a bath and trying to outwit that silly old tub was fun to me.

Another "different" thing about Chungking was that there were all kinds of insects everywhere. At night, they seemed to take over the entire city. Every Saturday we had to take our mattresses out of the house and beat the bugs out of them. Then we would try to kill the bugs with boiling water. One reason there were so many insects in the city, I suppose, was that many people cooked and ate right out on the street and left their scraps there also, without thinking about cleaning them up.

Soon after our arrival, my father began working as the doctor for employees in the Bank of China. At first, he had so few clothes to wear that I had to wash his shirts for him every day as soon as he got home so he would have clean shirts to wear the next day. (It was so hot in the city that he would carry an extra shirt to work to change into at noontime.)

The washing was done on a washboard and, since there was no electricity, the ironing had to be done with a heavy charcoal iron. It took me quite a while to learn how much charcoal to put into it and how to get the right temperature for ironing without scorching my father's shirts. But soon I could do more things without electricity than I had ever dreamed possible.

Going to school in Chungking presented a different kind of problem. Because it rained so much, I was always wading in mud halfway up to my knees most of the way to school. Worse yet, there were wild dogs in the fields, and I stayed terrified that a pack of them might attack me. When I walked home in the evenings, through streets that had no streetlights, I carried a flashlight, but sometimes the batteries would be dead before I could reach the house. It was scary.

My parents weren't too comfortable about the situation either, and soon they let me drop out of school temporarily until they could get me enrolled in a boarding school where there would be fewer hazards for me.

The day we moved from grandfather's house into our own home in Chungking was a happy day for me and my family. For the first time in years, we had a place to call our own.

Soon after we moved, my parents were able to enroll me in a Chinese boarding school conducted by American missionaries. There I learned more about the living Son of God who was already my invisible friend.

The school was a lot of fun for me. We sang many hymns, and we prayed our thanksgiving before every meal. It was easy for me to do that, because I was really grateful to have enough to eat. The devotional services in the evenings made me think about how wonderful God was. But I felt sad when we prayed about the friends we had left behind, and for our country that had been torn by war for so many years.

The dialect in Chungking was so different from what was spoken in Shanghai, it was almost like learning a new language. That made the songs, prayers, and every lesson at school quite a challenge to me. Once in a while, I would feel I was working very hard, and I would remember that long-ago promise to my mother that I would be a good girl so she could be proud of me.

"I would like to be your friend if you want me to."

"Who said that?" I asked, startled as I stood on the schoolground one day.

"I did," replied a girl who was standing behind me. Her name was Feng Yung Tat, and she was a senior in the school where I was in the seventh grade. Yung Tat soon became a great influence in my life. Her father was a famous general, Feng Yuk Cheung, and the whole family was devoutly Christian. I could tell that Yung Tat really loved the Lord. Every day she would tell me another wonderful story about Jesus and how much He loved me. Then we would pray together. I had thought I would be terribly lonely without my Shirley Temple doll to play with, but I soon forgot all about her. And I didn't even need the old man.

In so many ways, living in Chungking was like taking

up residence in an entirely different country. Some people even raised pigs right inside their homes! And the first time I noticed a group of men wearing funny white turbans around their heads, I thought they must be going to a funeral. But I found out they wore the turbans every day, because they believed that without them they would suffer severe headaches.

There were enough differences between the people of Shanghai and those of Chungking that some bitter feelings arose between the native citizens and the many refugees who were seeking asylum from the war-torn parts of our country. And soon Chungking was war-torn too. To everyone's great disappointment—but not surprise—the Japanese started bombing Chungking. Apparently they had not given up their hope of conquering all of China.

It was early afternoon when I first heard the eerie wail of the screaming air-raid sirens, and I thought all the demons of hell had been loosed upon us. Yung Tat grabbed my arm and screamed, "Run for your life, Neng Yee! The Japanese are coming to kill us!"

We ran, all right. Chungking is a city of mountain after mountain, and several blocks behind the school there was a mountain with a natural cave that had been enlarged and the walls shored up with planks to make an air-raid shelter. We crowded together inside, staying relatively close to the entrance so we wouldn't suffocate in the dead air far back in the cave.

With that first air raid, the nightmare of fear in which I had lived for so long was begun all over again. One after another the bombs screamed as they sought a target. Many people died in the streets. We could hear the cries of pain from those who didn't make it to the air-raid shelters in the hills. Sometimes those who died quickly were the lucky ones.

Most of the caves had no water or food, and often,

because of the large numbers crammed into them, people died of suffocation. Sometimes a bomb would drop so close to the entrance of the cave that people near the opening would be killed or injured. It was not uncommon for the blast from a bomb to seal the front of the cave, trapping its occupants in a living tomb. Many times I thought I would die in one of those shelters.

Once, the bombing did not stop for two and a half days. We were without water, food, and proper sanitation for all that time. The weather was hot, and the stench became almost unendurable.

Strangely, when the all-clear sounded, we would emerge from the caves and go about our daily business as if nothing out of the ordinary had happened. The bombings soon became an unpleasant but expected part of the routine of life.

In the summer of 1945, I was at home from school for a brief vacation when the impossible, longed-for news came on the radio at four o'clock in the afternoon:

JAPAN SURRENDERS!

Could it be true? Could the war be over at last? Could the hated Japanese be leaving the country we loved with all our hearts? Could we go home to Shanghai?

At first I couldn't believe that the Japanese would surrender to anyone. I had thought they would fight until the last man was dead and there was no Japan left to surrender.

It must be some kind of a trick, I decided.

But then my father came into the house, crying with joy:

"It's true! The evening paper has just come out! Look! The Japanese have surrendered!" We gathered around my father, peering over his shoulder at the words as he read the details aloud to us. Some of them were alarming, especially the part about the atomic bombs that had destroyed the cities of Hiroshima and Nagasaki. Almost everyone living in those places had been killed. That was terrible. But the atomic bomb had ended the war for millions more who would not have to die.

Everyone started to cry, even the most reserved among us. Some were crying for joy because the hope of returning to their homes and loved ones could be a reality after eight long years of wartime separation. For others, however, the tears were tears of sorrow, because the war had brought eternal separation from members of their families.

All night long the city of Chungking was aglow with fireworks. They were going off everywhere. No one could sleep or even tried to sleep—the excitement was wonderful.

In the midst of all the noise, I slipped off to be alone. I knew I had to thank the wonderful God for the end of the war. And I had to ask His help, too:

"God, please help me to return to my city of Shanghai, and some way, somehow, someday, help me to really get to know You."

If I could have guessed what was in store for me in Shanghai, I would have gone far in the other direction instead.

5

RETURNING

Peace! No more bombs! No more Japanese soldiers! No more running in fear! No more living in what was almost a foreign city to me!

I was eager to get back to my beloved Shanghai where my parents had promised I could go to the Mary Farnham School, run by Presbyterian missionaries. But there were no seats available on any flights from the Chungking airport for months. Then my mother remembered someone she knew in the military, and within a few weeks I was booked for a flight on a military plane bound for Nanking.

It was thrilling to watch our takeoff from the plane window and to realize that I was returning to a free Shanghai and a chance to study in one of the best schools in China. As we flew over the mountains, I remembered the misery we had all suffered there together just a few years earlier—the hunger, the cold, the pain. *But that is all in the past,* I told myself. *Now I have a wonderful new life ahead of me.*

If I had only known.

After we landed in Nanking, I caught the train to Shanghai where I was met by my mother's sister. As we drove to her home, we passed the house where I had lived with my grandmother. Cold chills ran down my back as I remembered those awful, lonely nights in the old dark wing. I wondered if the Buddhas still sat there, guarding the rotting meat.

A week later, I was enrolled in the Mary Farnham School. It was really two schools in one. On one side of the campus was the boys' school with their classrooms and dormitories, and on the other side of the campus was the girls' school with our classrooms and dormitories. Students never crossed the street between the two campuses except with special permission.

The school rated very high academically, and soon I found it difficult to keep up with the other girls my age, so I had to study very hard. We were approaching the time when we would have the examinations that would determine whether or not we would be permitted to go on to high school, and I wasn't sure that I could qualify.

And there was something else at the school that caught my attention more than academic matters. Almost every day I would hear someone say something about knowing God as their personal Savior. I wondered what they meant. It sounded like what I was wanting—to know God in an intensely personal way.

The chapel at school was open twenty-four hours a day, and I would often go there with the other girls to talk about Jesus and the Bible and to pray. I loved to hear them pray. When some of them talked to God, it sounded like they thought He was right there in the room with them. I longed to really know Him like my friends did, to know for certain that He heard and answered every prayer.

During my freshman year in school, when I was fourteen, just before the dreaded examination time, I saw a notice on the bulletin board that an American evangelist would be speaking on the boys' campus and that girls would be permitted to attend. Even though I felt I could not spare the time from my studies, I decided to get a pass from the matron and attend the meeting. None of my friends were going, because of the examinations scheduled for the next day. But I was so hungry for Jesus that I decided to go anyway. Somehow I sensed that getting an academic education wasn't the answer to all my needs. I didn't know exactly what I was seeking, but I had a feeling I could find it at that meeting.

Many of the girls were so concerned about their exams that they had their parents send them flashlights so they could study under their blankets after the official "lights out" at night. *Maybe I should call my mother and have her bring me a flashlight, too,* I thought. But then I reconsidered. After all, if I went to the meeting and really found God, He could provide everything I needed.

As I crossed the street to attend the meeting, I was amazed to realize that I wasn't worrying about the test. Since I didn't have a flashlight or candles to study by anyway, I might as well enjoy myself.

The moment I entered the auditorium and heard the singing, I *knew* God was there to be found.

"O God, please let me find You tonight." The prayer came from the bottom of my heart.

Soon I was sitting on the edge of my seat hearing the evangelist say, "Cast all your cares upon Him" and "For God so loved the world, that He gave His only begotten Son, that whosoever believes on Him should not perish but have eternal life."

Those words of God burned into my soul, and I knew that God did truly send Jesus to earth to bring me, Sung Neng Yee, to Him. He died on the cross, just for me. He had been rejected, just as I had been rejected so many times in my life.

When the evangelist invited everyone who wanted to accept Jesus as their personal Savior to come forward, I was on my feet. He didn't have to issue the invitation twice for me. This was what I had been yearning for for years, to know Jesus as my own.

With tears streaming down my cheeks and my body shaking like a leaf in a storm, I ran to the altar. The American preacher put his arm around my shoulders and leaned down close to my ear.

"My beloved, what do you want?" he asked me.

Sobbing it out, I said, "Do you—do you—do you think that this Jesus would want me? Can I have Jesus to be *my* Lord?"

Tears were in his eyes then too.

"Oh my child, my child," he sighed. "This is why I crossed the sea—just to tell you that Jesus is yours and that you belong to Him."

Then he helped me pray what he called a sinner's prayer, and he gave me the words to invite Jesus into my heart so I would know He was mine.

Afterward, I was floating on air. I didn't have to feel sorry for myself that I hadn't been accepted in my grandmother's house at her table—I was accepted in His house, at His table. I didn't have to think I was rejected because I didn't belong to anybody. I belonged to Him— the King of kings and the Lord of lords, the Creator of all that is! He loved me so much He had *died* for me!

I was so excited that when I walked back to the girls' campus, I felt like I owned the whole world. I was singing, laughing, and crying all at once, running over with joy. When I saw the school janitor making his rounds with his powerful flashlight in his hands, I asked him, "May I borrow your flashlight for tonight so I can study for my exams?" He didn't say no, he didn't ask me my name or what grade I was in, or explain that he couldn't do his job on the campus if he didn't have his light; he just looked at me and said, "Yes, you may use it," and handed it over.

I knew that was the Lord's provision for me, and I

almost laughed with joy all night as I studied beneath the blanket with my borrowed flashlight. I didn't just study, I also prayed that God would help me remember all the things I had worked so hard to learn. I knew that He heard my prayer because He was inside me, and the next day I passed all my examinations so I could enter the next year of high school.

A few weeks later, I proclaimed my new faith in Christ by being baptized. That was an important thing, because it would let everyone know I was a real Christian.

No one had told me that very soon it would be a dangerous thing to be a Christian anywhere in Mainland China.

But one very happy event occurred in the meantime.

My father's brother was a captain in the United States Army, serving as a dentist. He was often transferred from place to place, and he was stationed in Shanghai with his family for a brief period of time. When he got his orders to be transferred to Peking, his two-year-old son, Neng Yao, had the measles. The baby was too sick to travel safely in the cold weather, so they left him with my parents for the time being.

Soon after they moved to Peking, my aunt gave birth to a second son. Weeks turned into months, and still the two-year-old stayed with my family. It was lots of fun for me to pretend he was my little brother, and I would buy him clothes and dress him up, and even take him to school to visit with me.

One day my mother received a special delivery letter from my aunt.

"You may keep Neng Yao and make him your very own son," she wrote. "We have enough children without him."

There were no legal papers; the boy was just a gift of love from their family to ours. It is common in China, where one brother has two or more sons and another has none, for this kind of gift to be made, because it is considered so important for every family to have a son who can carry the head of the coffin when the father dies, as well as to have a son who can carry on the family name. And so my new brother brought much happiness to our family.

But soon the dark clouds came again, more terrible than any we had experienced before.

6

COMMUNISTS

The newly found peace that we were all enjoying was soon to end. A few short years after the end of the war, we started hearing talk about a movement called Communism. At first it sounded like a wonderful thing for China. But soon we began hearing rumors that made it sound worse than the most awful horrors of the Japanese occupation.

The thought of leaving our beloved Shanghai again was more than we could bear. But the sound of the guns made us realize that our days of safety were numbered. Every day the Communists were getting closer and closer to Nanking and the overthrow of our Nationalist government.

None of us really knew what the Communists stood for or just what would happen when and if they did take over the government. Some rumors said that the Communists would force girls to marry men not of their own choosing. Others said they would confiscate all our property. Still other rumors were of murder, Bible-burning, rape, atrocities. We chose not to believe them. But the rumors continued.

Rather than take a chance, many families started to leave the country. Some went to the United States, others to Hong Kong, still others fled to Taiwan. The poor had no choice but to remain and face whatever fate was theirs. Circumstances required many people of means to stay in their own country too.

My father said, "Well, we really don't have any place to go. We were raised in China, and none of our friends or relatives in the United States or Hong Kong have offered to help us. We will have to stay and see what happens."

If we had had any idea of what the next few years would hold for us, we'd have left that moment, forever, with only the clothes on our backs. But no one could have guessed. The horrors would be beyond imagination.

When my mother's sister and her husband took their children to the relative safety of Taipei, Taiwan, I decided to go to stay with them. My parents gave their consent, and in the winter of 1948 I boarded a freighter bound for Taipei. It took me three days to reach the island.

When I arrived, I was shocked at the conditions I found there. My beloved aunt's "apartment" was two rooms above an office—with no water or modern bathroom facilities. Worse yet, it was wintertime, and there was no heat in the building. All night long, all of us would huddle together on a quilt spread on the cold floor and try to keep from freezing to death.

A few such nights were enough to persuade me that the Communists couldn't be so bad after all. I missed my mother and my little brother, so I decided it would be better to risk the unknown with them than to stay in Taiwan. Within ten days, I was on another freighter headed for home.

Spring brought word of increasing Communist take-over, and by summer President Chiang Kai-shek's Nationalist government had left the Mainland to set up headquarters in Taipei.

I remember the night Shanghai fell into the hands of the Communists as though it were only moments ago.

Our house was close to the police station, and we could hear the intermittent staccato of machine guns driving their bullets all night—and then suddenly eerie, uninterrupted silence.

We learned that the police had been marched out of the building with their hands behind their heads, and the Communists had marched in. Next, they took over the radio station and the airport. Everything stopped that day. The Communists were in power.

Because none of us really knew the Communists and what they stood for, we were totally unprepared for what came next. Many people were blinded by their propaganda. Leaflets, newspapers, and magazines flooded the country, heralding a new age, the new freedom of Communism. I was in my second year in high school, and observed that our books and teaching materials took on a Communistic approach almost immediately. There were gradual changes in the community, too. American movies were stopped, and all the old officialdom was removed to make way for the new regime. Doctors couldn't be trained overnight, however, and so my father was permitted to continue with his practice at first.

The nightmare of terror really began on the eve of the 1950 Chinese New Year. That morning, people went out innocently to greet one another as always, to bow and smile to each other, wishing each a wonderful New Year. But that day, when we stepped outside, our eyes were confronted with ugly posters the Communists had stuck all over windows and doors, on fences and the sides of buildings.

"You dirty dogs," the most polite of them proclaimed, "you deserve to die."

We didn't know we had done anything wrong, but they seemed to think so. Before the day was over there were riots, and bodies were left lying in the streets. We were baffled. What was it all about?

Within a few days, word came that my father had been arrested and imprisoned on the top floor of the hospital. No one could visit him, and he was not allowed to come home. Day after day, night after night, he was interrogated by the authorities. After two weeks, he was released, and our home was confiscated to repay "the debt" they said he owed to the people for stealing money from the hospital. It was all a lie, of course, but we had no opportunity to prove anything.

Gathering together what belongings we could carry, we became refugees again in our own city. In a squalid slum factory district, we were assigned to a single little room attached to the side of an old building that was almost falling down. Walls were crumbling, windows were broken out, there was no sign that anything had ever been painted—but we had nowhere else to go. Five other families shared the "house" with us, and we used the same kitchen with all of them. There was no bathroom.

The Communists put my father to work as a doctor in a factory. There he was forced to diagnose and treat over a hundred patients a day, and we were given a small amount of money to buy food.

At that time I was attending the law school at Soochow University, being brainwashed by the Communist professors. Although the school had been a Christian school, all religious activity had stopped with the coming of the Communists. We heard that ministers and priests were being imprisoned, punished, or killed. Some simply disappeared. No one dared to mention the name of God.

It is hard to believe, but soon we became accustomed to these things and lived as if they were not happening.

One day while I was a student at Soochow, I noticed a young man on the campus. He was very tall and good looking, and I was so attracted by his outward appearance that it didn't occur to me that other qualities were perhaps more important than good looks. My girlfriends told me he played the piano very well, and that he was quiet and reserved. When they told me also that he had never been known to date a girl on the campus, I was challenged. Although I didn't know his name or address, I bet them I could get a date with him within two weeks' time.

Since he was a senior and I was only a junior, we were not in any of the same classes, so I had to make opportunities to meet him and engage him in conversations in the library or study hall. I learned that his name was Lam Kai Sing, and from the beginning I sensed there was something very different about him. He often seemed sad and melancholy, and he had negative ideas about many things. But I persuaded myself that if he had problems, I could love him enough to overcome them all.

If I can only get him to marry me, I thought, *then everything will be all right.* Oh, if only I had asked the Lord for His plan instead of being bent so determinedly on pursuing my own. But I had stopped praying, I had stopped reading the Bible, there was no church service to attend, and I was living as if I had never met the Lord at all.

When a mutual friend told me that Kai Sing was planning a trip to Hong Kong, the city we all regarded as a shopper's paradise, I went to his apartment to see him. The family maid opened the door and let me in. When Kai Sing came out to speak to me, I told him I had heard of his upcoming trip to Hong Kong and that I wanted him to make a purchase there for me. He agreed to do it, so I handed him the money, ignoring the fact that he was being very polite and cold about it.

Then I told him I had tickets to a concert that would be held in a few days, and would be pleased if he would accompany me as payment for the favor he had agreed to do for me.

"Let's have dinner together first," he said, "and then we can go to the concert afterward."

I had already won my bet with my girlfriends. Even

better, I had learned that what came across as coldness in Kai Sing might just be a kind of shyness, a fear that someone might reject him. I could certainly relate to someone like that.

I'll never forget how Kai Sing looked when we met in the restaurant on the night of the concert. He had on a pink sharkskin suit without a wrinkle in it anywhere. The food could have been mud, the concert only a raucous racket for all I knew. I had eyes and ears only for Kai Sing.

While he was in Hong Kong, I went to his Shanghai apartment several times to get acquainted with his maid, and we became good friends. Kai Sing wrote me several long letters while he was away, and after his return to Shanghai he continued to write me, since he had graduated but I was still in school.

Everyone who knew both of us told me that Kai Sing and I were exact opposites in temperament. I woke up cheerful and ready to go every morning—outgoing, almost like a full-time cheerleader. Kai Sing, they said, was moody all the time, like someone who had already dropped dead. But I couldn't see it. To me, he was perfect, and I was determined to win him.

We dated each other for four years, and still he wasn't interested in getting married because he was so pessimistic about the future. He had been sick with tuberculosis as a young boy, and sometimes he thought he wouldn't live very long. That's why he didn't want to take on the added responsibility of a wife, he said. But I told him I didn't care about that, nor about the low salary he received working in the court. I could supplement that with my teaching salary, I told him. Besides, it didn't matter to me how we lived—just so we lived with each other.

By 1955, I was tired of not getting married, so I told him I was going to drop his friendship. Maybe that would get a little action out of him. To my surprise, he went to my father and threatened to kill himself if I stopped seeing him. My father encouraged me to marry him, but how could I talk him into it?

Finally I decided that if I would sleep with him and get pregnant, *then* he would marry me. At the first sign that I might be expecting a baby, I went to a doctor who took my pulse and nodded his head.

"Yes, you're pregnant."

As soon as I told Kai Sing that I was expecting his child, he loved the baby.

"Let's get married right away," he said, as happy as I was for once.

My parents printed the traditional red invitations to announce the marriage to all their friends, and on July 1, 1955, we had a big wedding supper in the Chinese restaurant at the Ging Jung Hotel. There were five big round tables full of guests, and my father made a speech. Then everyone toasted the bridal couple so they would have long life and happiness together. We spent our wedding night in the little curtained-off bed corner of my parents' "home." My aunt had helped me make the bed, tucking into the folds of the sheets a dozen brightly painted red eggs, following the traditional custom to ensure fertility to the union. She didn't know that in our case the custom was unnecessary because I was already expecting our first baby.

I had set out to get what I wanted, and I got it.

And then, within less than a month, persecution came for me. The day when eight Communist sharpshooters raised their rifles and took careful aim at me. The day when I heard the bullets whining toward me. The day when I fell to the ground.

7

A NEW LIFE

For a few seconds I lay motionless, just like the bodies in the field around me. Was this all there was to dying? The air was silent, except for the echo of shots still reverberating in the dusk.

Then a startling realization hit me—

I was breathing!

I wasn't dead!

I was alive!

But how could it be? What about the shots—the whine of bullets coming straight toward me? Communist sharpshooters never missed. What had happened?

The force of my fall had somehow loosened the ropes that tied my hands, and I wriggled them free and sat up, pulling the blindfold from my eyes. Yes, I could see. . . . I looked down at my clothes—no bullet holes, no blood. I felt of my body—no new pain, no bullet-inflicted injury.

I *was* alive!

By then the Communists were jerking me to my feet, shoving me back in the direction of the school. Anger, frustration, and bewilderment contorted their faces. A short distance away, the firing squad stood as if it were frozen in place—or turned to stone—looking at me dumbfounded, as if they doubted I was real.

The next thing I knew, we were back in the interrogation room again, the questions angrier than ever:

"WHY DID THE BULLETS COME OUT FROM THE GUNS AND GO OVER YOU AND UNDER YOU AND AROUND YOU, BUT NONE HIT YOU?!?!?

"WHAT WAS THE LIGHT THAT CAME DOWN FROM THE SKY AND BLINDED US SO WE COULDN'T SEE YOU?!?!?!?"

I knew the answer to that one.

"Jesus is the Light," I said.

"DON'T PREACH AT US!"

"I'm not preaching. I'm telling the truth, answering your question."

Their senseless, furious, insane screaming went on for hours—old questions, new questions. But in the midst of them all I had perfect peace. I was alive! And the quiet words I was hearing above the noise of my thundering persecutors were words from the Lord, words that promised, "Whosoever will save his life shall lose it: and whosoever will lose his life for My sake shall find it." I didn't understand how it had happened, but I knew that because I had been willing to lose my life for Jesus, I had found my life instead. I was thankful.

By three o'clock in the morning, all my tormentors were exhausted, so I was thrown into a guarded room and allowed to rest. I slept like a baby, and as I slept I dreamed God spoke to me. He told me not to be afraid, that I and all my family would get out of Red China someday.

I didn't see how His promise could be true, but I knew it was, because God could not lie.

The next day my teaching job was taken away from me, and there was a new meeting, with more screaming accusations, more probing questions, more slapping, spitting, and cursing at me. But no one tried to kill me again. And after a few more days, they even let me go home for the night.

I didn't tell Kai Sing or my father about the firing squad. They were already being persecuted so continually themselves that I could see they were near the breaking point. I did tell my mother, though, because I had to talk to someone. She was so frightened already that one more incident could not increase her fear. Maybe it would even give her hope when she learned that God had heard my prayer and saved me and my baby from the bullets in some miraculous way.

When I told her, she was too numb to say anything, and afraid to cry out loud, but I could read the awful hurt in her eyes and the love that was too deep for words. When I said God had promised me that our whole family would escape from Red China, she only smiled wistfully and shook her head as if it could never be so. It was too much for her to believe.

Saying goodbye to mother the next morning was like saying goodbye forever.

"Mom, I don't know if I will ever see you in this world again, but don't be afraid. Never deny Jesus, and if this is my last day, we will certainly meet in heaven."

Yes, I believed God's promise, but freedom seemed impossibly far away.

Although I was no longer permitted to teach, I had to ride the Shanghai bus to school every morning early to face more persecution and brainwashing. At school, I was a marked person, avoided like a leper. Everyone was understandably afraid to be associated with me. Nobody would speak to me—except my tormentors.

Sometimes I would be permitted to take the bus back home at six or seven o'clock at night; sometimes I wouldn't be released until eleven, when the buses had already stopped for the night. When it was late, sometimes I would find an old ricksha man and pay him to let me sit on the uncomfortable rack on the back of his bicycle for the hour-long, painful, bumpy ride to the place where my family was staying. Sometimes, for weeks at a time, the Communists would make me spend the night in the school, sleeping on the dirty concrete floor of the classroom with no blanket, no food, no chance to bathe or wash my clothes.

I almost never saw my husband or father, because they were often required to spend the night at their places of employment—my father at the hospital and my judge-husband at the court. The Communists were careful not to let all three of us be at home at the same time very often. They didn't want non-Communists to communicate with one another.

The days were full of mental and physical torture for us all, fear, suspicion, confusion. We no longer thought about such trivial, unimportant things as what we would eat or where we would sleep or whether or not we felt comfortable. All we could do was pray that the Lord would strengthen us for whatever we had to bear.

I knew the Bible said that where two agreed together in the name of Jesus, God would answer their prayers. But when I was locked up in the school with five thousand other students and professors, and all of us were afraid to speak to one another, I couldn't find another person to make two. Then the Lord reminded me that I was pregnant with my first baby, and that the baby and I together made two.

"In the name of Jesus," I said to my unborn child, "you and I are two. And we're going to agree that we are going through this trial together. I don't have any food to feed you, baby, and I don't know how long it will be, but you have got to fight this battle along with me. In the name of Jesus."

And we prayed, oh how we prayed! And somehow, God sustained us.

Many days I was required to spend the whole day writing my life story, from the day I was born, telling everything I had ever known about my parents, their background, my relatives, their friends, my teachers, my adopted brother, everyone else I had ever known, how and when I met them, what they did for a living, what they thought about Communism, who their friends were and what they did . . .

There was no end to the material I was supposed to write. And I had to put my fingerprints on all of it to prove the words were mine.

I had to tell the truth, because I knew that sooner or later I would be forced to write on the same topics again, and I would not be able to remember lies. If there was any discrepancy between what I said one time and what I said another time, I would be in for it.

The Communists were never satisfied with the material I had written.

"It's too short!" they'd scream. Or "It's too long! It's not clear! We don't understand! It's not true!" There was no way to satisfy them; they would always pick everything to pieces. And then, always, came the insatiable demand, "Write it all again! Write it from the beginning! Don't pretend you don't know! Tell us everything!"

They never let me have a copy of what I had written to help me because they wanted to find inconsistencies to trap me at the next interrogation session.

I felt like an empty tube of toothpaste, being squeezed and squeezed to get more out of me when there was nothing left.

At irregular intervals I would be relieved of the writing chore temporarily to be dragged into a large room and put under a spotlight for questioning about all I had written. The Communists would come at me with their screaming, almost crushing me as they crowded around. It seemed there were thousands of them, all yelling at once, threatening to kill my mother or father or husband or brother if I didn't give them the answers they wanted. And then, to see if they could break me another way, they would put me in a small room with only one other person, someone with a soft, confidential voice, trying to persuade me to make a confession and betray a friend.

Repeatedly, I would be without food or water for days at a time. And then, for no apparent reason, they would let me go home for the night.

I often wondered what effect all the mental and physical torture was having on my unborn baby. I was far more concerned about the life of the child in my womb than I was about my own.

During the days when I was locked in a room by myself, writing material and more material, Jesus grew exceedingly precious to me. As I prayed, agreeing with my child, I could feel His love surround me, and the fear and loneliness would drain away. I would rest on His promise of deliverance—someday—and trust Him to guide my thoughts for what I was to write on the paper. In these hours, I would tell the baby within me that God loved him and cared for him. Then I would cry to the Lord not to let my child be harmed.

I was sleeping at home on the night of February 14 when I was awakened by the beginning of labor pains. A maid got a pedicab and went with me to the hospital. The doctor who examined me was very gruff.

"First babies take a long time," he growled. Then he sent me to a cold hallway where I had to sit in a chair for the rest of the night before anyone located a bed for me.

The next day my mother and her sister came to the hospital to visit and stayed beside me for many hours, but the baby didn't come. They returned the next day and the next. Still no baby. I was in an agony of pain and begged the nurses to help me, but they seemed not to care. I feared I was bleeding to death and that the baby was dying too.

When I had been in labor seventy-two hours, one of the nurses told me the baby's head was too large for the birth canal and that the baby should have been delivered by Caesarean section, but it was too late to do that now.

When I asked what could be done, she shrugged her shoulders and turned away, as if she wanted both of us to die. Not caring what happened to me, concerned only that my baby have a chance to live, I summoned all the strength remaining in me and literally forced the baby from my body with a mighty effort and tearing, rending pain.

"It's a boy," I heard someone say, dispassionately, "and he's all right—a healthy, well-formed child."

Tears of joy and relief flooded my cheeks as I silently prayed my thanksgiving. Truly God was a God of miracles, for I had delivered a healthy son. In that moment, I gave him to God to be His servant.

And finally I slept.

8

THREE GOODBYES

I had had my baby, but I knew I'd have to face the Communists again after my fifty-six-day leave for childbirth was over. When I was discharged from the hospital, I felt so weak that I didn't know how I could take care of myself, let alone take care of a baby. I didn't even know how to change a diaper. How thankful I was to have my mother's help! And in my heart, I knew that somehow God would continue to take care of us all.

About two months after I came home from the hospital, I received word that I was to report to school again. Every morning after feeding little Chuin Man and changing him, I had to rush to catch the bus and submit myself to day-long questioning. Sometimes I would be allowed to go home at night, sometimes they would insist on keeping me at school for several days and nights in a row, in spite of the fact that I was nursing my baby. Being forced to stay away from him for days at a time was very painful to me, and of course my milk was soon gone. Then I had a new problem—where to find milk to feed my baby.

Like everything else, milk was hard to get. The Communists were exporting milk powder and not leaving enough for the Chinese people. Every morning I would have to take the few pennies I had, go far from home to find milk on my way to school, and pay the girl who took up tickets on the bus to take the milk to my mother for the baby. Fortunately, we lived near the end of the bus line, and the ticket girl was able to do this for me. Somehow, little Chuin Man managed to survive.

Before long, I was expecting a second child, and I found it hard to bear the thought of bringing another baby into this life of misery and wretched trials. There was never enough to eat. We were allotted only one small bottle of oil each month for the whole family, four ounces of meat and twenty pounds of rice for one person. Sometimes when I would come home from school to our cold room and see my mother holding Chuin Man, trying to keep him warm, I would cry, "Lord, how will we ever make it with another baby?"

Bad as they were, things were about to get worse for our family—much worse.

One day one of our friends came to us and reported that, although my father had never taken any part in politics, the Communists had summoned him to a large political meeting and forced him to stand on a little chair for twenty-four hours while they questioned him about everything they could think of. It was one of their favorite methods of torture.

"Why was your father so rich?—Why did you study in France?—How do you feel about Communism?—Why are you acquainted with Catholics? . . ."

It was not enough that they had taken away his job, his car, his house, his furniture, that they had sent him to a hovel to live and given him a backbreaking job as a factory physician, that they questioned him incessantly, trying to break his mind and spirit. They were about to devise a new method of torture especially for him.

Because the wind and rain poured into our home in bad weather, it was not surprising that he contracted a bad case of influenza and had to be hospitalized "for observation and treatment," as they called it. When we received word of his illness, I went at once to visit him. It seemed to me afterward that "for torture and annihilation" would have been a more accurate description of the purpose of his hospitalization.

One day as I bathed his feet, trying to make his raging fever subside, I heard him sigh and say quietly, so only I could hear, "Oh, how I wish I could be out of here for just one day! Oh, for a single day's holiday from all this torment!"

I joined my yearnings to his, and said, "Oh, yes, Dad. Maybe we couldn't have a picnic, and we couldn't go for a ride since we have no car now, but it would be so wonderful just to have you at home so we could all sit and talk together."

We started planning what we would do when he was well enough to get out of the hospital and before he had to go back to work. And there came a day, finally, when the fever was all gone. He still looked sick because he was badly undernourished and had a persistent cough, but since the fever was gone, I was confident the doctors would allow him to come home. In fact, I asked permission to spend the night beside his bed so I would be on hand if they let him go the next morning before my mother came to visit him.

During the dark quiet hours, my father said, "Neng Yee, listen closely to what I have to say. I want to tell you something very important."

When I had drawn my chair closer to the bed and was leaning near his pillow, he whispered, "They are testing some kind of new medicine on me, a medicine from Russia."

"Why would they do that? Why would they test a new medicine on a doctor? You're already getting over your influenza without it."

"I don't know," he said, "but a trusted Communist doctor gave me the medicine this morning. He said he didn't know exactly what was in it himself, just something new they were trying. And I noticed that after a few hours I began to hemorrhage from my bowels . . ."

I didn't wait to hear the rest of it; I called for a nurse immediately and insisted he be given a blood transfusion. After the transfusion, he began to suffer from terrible thirst, but the doctor had left orders he was not to have anything to drink, so I talked him out of it, thinking the new medicine might be designed to have him on his feet the next day.

Before I left for home, knowing my mother was already on her way to take my place beside his bed while I spent the day at school, he said to me, "Neng Yee, if you ever have any trouble, remember you can always go to America. Those blue-eyed, green-eyed, black and white people are Christians. They will love you."

"Yes, Dad," I told him. "I will never forget."

It took me an hour and a half to get home. When I walked in the door, the phone was ringing. It was my mother.

"They stopped me at the door of the hospital as soon as I got here," she said. "They told me I should call the family immediately—your father is in critical condition."

My brother and I hurried to the hospital as fast as we could get there. But we were too late. When the three of us walked into his room together, the sheet had already been drawn up over his face. I turned it back, and saw to my horror that the sheets were drenched with blood that had poured from every opening in his body.

"Look!" I screamed. "He didn't die—he was murdered!"

I insisted that the Communists admit it before we held the funeral. Of course, it was unthinkable that someone as young as I was, and not a Communist, could force them to do anything, but I stood my ground. My mother was weeping. I had never seen her cry before.

At the funeral parlor, after the morticians had cut his hair and given him a bath and put him in the viewing room, I repeated my ultimatum. If no one confessed to his murder with medicine that was really a deadly poison, causing him to bleed to death, I would not permit the funeral to begin. Because another funeral was scheduled for a little later in the day, the funeral director was eager to get us out of the way. But I continued to insist the service could not begin until full confession was made.

Finally I got my way. The doctor who had given my father the medication appeared and explained that the medicine was for heart trouble and rheumatism. My father had neither of those conditions, and yet the doctor had followed his orders to test the new drug on my father. He had accidentally given him too much, he said, and that is what had led to his death. In my heart, of course, I knew the overdose had been given on purpose. But when the doctor made the admission, I said, "All right. You may begin the funeral now." Then, at last, I broke down and cried.

A month before the death of my father, my second child, a daughter, was born. Oh, how I longed to get her, my son, my husband, and my mother out of the country and away from the Communists before it was too late. But how could I do it?

"Please God, my father is gone, my mother isn't well, my husband is being persecuted, and I can't get enough food for my babies. Please God, make a way of escape!"

There was more I could have told Him, about how my husband had begun to have violent rages, hurling dishes against the wall, slapping my face. But I was sure God already knew all about it. I rationalized that his erratic behavior was one of his reactions to the Communist oppression.

"And when we all get out of Red China, everything will be wonderful," I told myself, only half believing it.

By the time my baby girl, Chuin Way, was a year old, I was desperate. We were all hungry all the time. Food was so limited that I feared we would all die of starvation.

"Jesus, what can we do?"

"Would you believe Me for one thing?"

"Yes, Lord. For what?"

"Trust Me for only one day at a time, Neng Yee. If you really believe Me, you must send your daughter to your mother-in-law in Hong Kong."

"But, Lord—"

"You must listen to My voice and take one step at a time. Don't worry about the rest. Just obey."

There was no way a baby could travel alone, but the Lord put it in the heart of her nanny, Yee Ah Hsing, to go with her to Hong Kong, even though she had a son of her own, a mother-in-law, and a husband in Mainland China. I was amazed! It had to be the hand of God to make a way for what He had told me to do.

I applied for their exit permits, and in three weeks they had permission to go to Hong Kong. I went with them as far as Canton—two days and three nights by train. The nanny had taken care of my baby more than I had. But during those days and nights on the train, Chuin Way must have sensed she was going to leave me, because she clung so tightly around my neck that I had to push her away so she could get on the boat for Macao. How hard it was for me to see her go!

I said goodbye to both of them and stood crying after they left. They had been gone only a few minutes when they returned, so the nanny could hand a small gold cross to me that had been around the baby's neck. The

Communists would not permit anyone to take gold out of the country, she said. We all cried again, and then they were gone, this time not to return.

I felt I had passed the first test for getting my whole family out of China. Soon I realized I would have to get my husband out of the country next.

The Communists had been against him from the beginning, because he was from a wealthy Hong Kong family and had a good education. They had been persecuting him for two years already, often making him stay all night at the court, questioning him day in and day out as they had my father and me. Then, a few months after my daughter had left for Hong Kong, men from the court where Kai Sing worked had come to say that the Communists were planning to assign him to a labor camp.

"All educated people should have experience at hard labor," they said.

I had heard some things about those labor camps. It was not just that the work was hard, but the conditions under which people were forced to work would kill a man in good health, and Kai Sing had never been strong. One of his brothers was already dying with tuberculosis, and I knew that if Kai Sing had to go to a labor camp, he would never survive.

I wrote to my mother-in-law and told her the situation. "I would rather have your son live with you than have him stay with me and die in a labor camp under the Communists," I said.

She wrote back that Kai Sing's father was actually critically ill with a liver disease and the doctors didn't expect him to live very long. That seemed a good reason for the Communists to grant permission for Kai Sing to visit his father for a month or so. As long as he left his wife and son behind, the Communists would know that he would return, especially since I was obviously expecting our third child very soon.

Out of all the men working in the court system who wanted to get out of Red China at that time, Kai Sing was the only one who received permission to go. I packed his clothes, and Chuin Man and I went to the train station to see him off.

"I don't know if I'll see you again while I'm still in my twenties," I told him, "or when I'm thirty or forty or fifty, but we'll meet again someday. Please wait for me."

Then I asked him to send me a telegram as soon as he reached Hong Kong asking me to join him there for the birth of our baby. I thought I could use such a telegram as the basis to request an exit permit that would allow Chuin Man and me to get out of Red China and join him in a few weeks.

I couldn't have been more wrong!

It was May 8, and as I stood holding Chuin Man in my arms, watching the train move slowly out of the station, I felt like a knife was cutting my heart. Policemen and Communist soldiers were standing all around, so I dared not cry. I felt a deep loneliness settle on me as the train moved away and was soon out of sight. The tears I had not allowed to show on the outside were flowing inside me.

When I got home that night, there was a call from the school telling me to return to work at once.

9

DELIVERANCE

I was eight-and-a-half-months pregnant. Because of poor nutrition and other factors, I was so swollen with fluid I weighed over two hundred pounds. My kidneys were infected, my liver was infected, and my whole system was in such bad shape from repeated whippings and scaldings that sometimes I could just touch my skin and the blood would spill out.

Despite the fact that I was in this terrible condition, the Communists said they had a surprise for me:

"What you need is some heavy labor. It will be good for you physically, and it will teach you that even the cultured and well-educated must work alongside the peasant for the success of the Communist cause. It will be especially good for you because you are expecting a child.

"The work is hard."

For once, they were telling the truth. The work *was* hard.

Early the next morning, I was crowded into the back of a big truck loaded with students and teachers assigned to the labor camp so they would not think intellectualism was the only way to help the Communist cause.

The ride on the back of the big truck as it swerved and bumped over the rocky road was almost more than I could endure. But the worst was yet to come. When the truck ground to a halt, we were ordered to climb down, and I saw before me a massive mountain of coal that towered higher than a ten-story building. Moving that mountain was our assignment. Moving it by hand.

The Communists gave each of us a bamboo pole to put across our shoulders, and two bamboo baskets to load with coal and carry to a waiting truck until it was filled. Then we would load another truck in the same manner— day after day, week after week, month after month. Without food, water, or a chance to rest.

My heart sank.

"Lord, already I can hardly walk because my body is so swollen. How am I going to walk with a load of coal hanging from each shoulder?"

He seemed to say, "Do not be worried or upset. If you have a mustard seed of faith, you can move any mountain. Nothing is too hard for Me. I would never let you have a burden that was more than you could carry."

His reassurance made me determined not to be weak, but to be an example.

The Communists weighed out two baskets of coal the size they wanted me to carry—their combined weight was 130 pounds!

Wearing flimsy shoes made of thin boards with rags wrapped around them, without gloves, without a hat to protect my head from the hundred degree temperature, I set to work. The sun burned my face until it blistered and peeled, leaving painful sores from sun poisoning. My hands were cut and bleeding, coal dust filling every pore. My shoes fell apart, and my feet were bruised and blistered. Each step along the narrow splintery board between coal and truck was sheer torture. But if I slowed down, the Communists used a long whip to speed me up. The days were hell from beginning to end. But I knew that I would soon have relief because the Communists allowed a woman to take fifty-six days from her job for childbirth, and it was almost time for my baby to be born.

When my husband had left Red China, I had asked him to send me a telegram from Hong Kong as soon as possible, asking me to join him for the birth of the baby. I had used the telegram as a basis to apply for an exit permit. The local authorities had accepted my application, but indicated that there was no hope for my release since I was their guarantee that my husband would return to the country after visiting his sick father. In the natural, my release seemed impossible, but I knew that nothing is impossible with God. And my heart remained full of expectancy at what He would do.

My back was in such pain from the constant walking with all the weight of the coal added to my own weight that at night I couldn't lie down to rest. Instead, I would sit on the floor and cry out to God, asking for a release from my suffering.

"Lord, let me get out of Red China," I cried. "I yearn to be in a land that's free. You promised . . ."

Suddenly He spoke to me:

"Neng Yee, I'm with you. I'm almighty, the One who gives you life. Trust Me. If I am for you, who can be against you?"

"Give me a sign, Lord. Life is so hard—give me a sign."

"As long as the baby is in your womb, I am with you. Your baby will be a son, and he will not be born in Red China; he will be born in Hong Kong."

That meant I would be in a free land very soon! I touched my body and dedicated the baby to the Lord. I dedicated the other children too, and made a new commitment of my own life.

The next morning, I reported to the labor camp with new hope. God's promise was my sustenance as each new day dawned with its hours of torture and excruciating pain.

The hard labor of the coal field was daily becoming more difficult for me. I weighed 235 pounds now, and looked more like an animal than a human being. Every morning, when I arrived at the field, I would say, "Mountain, be removed in the name of Jesus." At night I would sit on the floor beside my bed and cry softly so as not to disturb my mother.

Many people died in the labor camps because of the awful heat—one hundred degrees in the shade, only there was no shade. The humidity hovered around ninety percent.

When I cried out for water, the Communists splashed boiling water on my face and added to my misery. When people fainted, their bodies would be picked up and loaded on a truck. Any that had not revived by the time the truck arrived at the site of a common grave were covered with earth by big bulldozers—dead or alive.

Almost every day I checked with police at the Shanghai station to see if my exit permit had come through. The answer was always no. May went by, June, July, and the beginning of August . . .

I was nearly twelve months pregnant!

The Lord spoke to me again:

"Neng Yee, the baby is alive and well in your womb. And I am with you. Continue to trust in Me."

I *was* trusting Him, and meanwhile, I had also done my part to win favor with the local authorities so there would be no holdup when the time came for me to leave the country. A recommendation from one's place of work was required for an exit permit, and I had won the friendship of the principal of the school in several ways. When she had a new baby, I had sent my maid to her house to help wash diapers—the Communists were not allowed to hire servants of their own. And when the school had a large quota of government bond sales to fill, I bought bonds with the money my mother-in-law had sent me when my first two children were born. That made the school look good, and the principal was grateful. When the local police, whose station was across the alley from the place where I was living, wanted to heat milk to drink, we let them use our "community kitchen." They all loved Chuin Man and liked to play ball with him outside.

I had everyone on my side except the Shanghai central police, who were in control of the whole matter. I would have to find some way to overcome their opposition.

One day my patience with them ran out.

I decided to go to the central telephone company office where I could make a long-distance call to my husband in Hong Kong. I told him all about the torture of the labor camp, and I shouted, "How come the Communists tell the whole world we have freedom, but they won't let me get out of Red China so my baby can be born?" I was so angry I ranted and raved for almost half an hour on long distance telephone. Everyone in the office heard me.

I knew it might be dangerous for me to criticize the government, but I was so angry I didn't care whether it was dangerous or not.

When I hung up the telephone, I sent telegrams to Communist Party Chairman Mao Tse-Tung and to Premier Chou En-Lai, who was responsible for exit permit approvals at that time. I was literally storming Peking.

"You say we are a free people," I said in the telegrams, "and yet you are holding me captive when I desire to join my husband in Hong Kong for the birth of my child. Please ask the Shanghai authorities to hurry and grant my exit permit so I can be free to use my fifty-six days for my baby to be born . . ."

The telegram was as long as a letter, because I wanted to be sure to get my point across. Every day I checked with the police station about my exit permit, and every day I sent another telegram to Peking. It was very expensive to send all those telegrams. I sold a few pieces of my father's furniture to pay for them, certain he would have approved.

One Tuesday morning in August, I had to go by the school to see someone before reporting to the labor camp. As I waited in the office, the Lord spoke to me in a strong, clear voice:

"Neng Yee, the way is now open for you to get out of Red China."

I ran across the street to a telephone. First, I called my mother. Someone answered the phone for her, because she had been in bed for months with heart trouble, but she was able to come to the phone and talk with me.

"Mom! I'm leaving tomorrow! The Lord just told me. And later, He will provide the way for you so we can all be together again."

Next, I checked with the only airline. They had two flights from Shanghai to Canton—one leaving on Wednesday, the other on Friday. I booked space for Chuin Man and me on the Wednesday flight that would leave the very next day.

Then I called the central police station. I recognized the voice of the man who answered the phone, identified myself, and asked him if my exit permit had arrived.

He was angry—as usual—and berated me for disturbing him.

"If you want to know anything, don't call. Come in this afternoon at four o'clock."

But the Lord told me, "Go now. It's urgent."

When I walked into the station, I said, "I want my exit permit."

The Chief of Police himself came out to deal with me.

"Have you any idea how much trouble you're giving us?" he demanded. "What's the meaning of all those telegrams you've been sending to Peking? You have embarrassed our office and caused unwanted criticism and attention to fall on our heads. Forty telegrams! It's unheard of! So now Peking is checking up on Shanghai to find out why we haven't allowed you to leave. You have put us in a bad spot. And now you say you have reserved tickets for yourself and your son! How do you know you're going to be able to use them?"

"Because I have faith in the living God and know He is able to do everything," I replied.

That set him off into even greater fury.

"First we don't understand why the bullets didn't kill you! Now we don't understand why this baby isn't born yet! We don't want such things—miracles"—he said the word with a sneer of contempt—"to happen in our country." Then he gave me a look of utter disgust and threw the exit permits at me with a word of warning:

"Usually we take steps to ensure that someone who leaves the country will return, but your case is different. We demand that you get out—and stay out—forever!"

I stooped to pick up the vital pieces of paper. I didn't thank the man who was puffing his furious indignation at me, but I did thank the living Lord.

"Jesus," I said under my breath, "I will live for You the rest of my life. Don't let Neng Yee live any more, but You live in me."

On the way home I went to the bank and got the money I would need for the trip from my safe-deposit box. I knew I couldn't take any valuables out of the country with me, so I left everything else in the box for my mother. As soon as I got home, I gathered a few pieces of clothing for myself and for Chuin Man, and made a small bundle of them. Then I said goodbye to my fourteen-year-old brother and to my ailing mother.

How hard it was to leave them! I couldn't have done it if I hadn't been certain it was God's plan and that He would bring them out later, in the perfect time.

My brother wasn't old enough to be really aware of the significance of my leaving. He told me only not to wake him up when I left early in the morning. Mother, however, was a different matter. She had been in bed so long that she feared she would never be well enough to get out of the country.

"But Jesus has promised," I reminded her. "I know He will allow us to be together again."

I was grateful that she didn't cry, but my own tears were a flood all the way to the airport.

The flight to Canton in a small plane took about six hours. The next lap of the journey was by taxi and a number of little boats across many winding rivers before we reached the border. There the Communists searched through the pitiful little bundle I would carry across no man's land. They found nothing worth confiscating except for my wedding ring on my finger. I would not be allowed to take that out of the country, they said, but they would mail it back to my mother.

As little Chuin Man and I began to stumble across the unkempt, deserted stretch of land separating tyranny from freedom, I was filled with praise to God, and yet I was so exhausted physically and emotionally that the relatively short distance—it couldn't have been over a mile or so—seemed almost insurmountable. It was hot, the ground was rocky, and my enormous size made every step excruciatingly painful. Chuin Man was hungry and thirsty, but there was nothing I could do for him. Branches and sharp-twigged bushes soon had our legs scratched and bleeding. Both of us fell down several times. And when blood began flowing from my body, I was sure my baby was about to be born there in the middle of the wilderness, with no one to help me. If that happened, I knew we would die.

"O living God, please help me to go on! Or am I to die right here?"

"How little faith you have," an inner voice chided.

"The same God who has let you carry this baby for all this time is not about to forsake you now."

"I have a job for you to do—and for your son," the Lord seemed to say, affirming His everlasting faithfulness.

I felt little Chuin Man tugging at my arm, as if he could pull me up from where I had fallen. The tiny determined tug helped me receive God's strength for what remained of the journey. When Chuin Man became tired and begged me to carry him, I could only look at him with love in my eyes and pray that God would give his tired little legs the strength to push on.

Finally we could see Macao ahead—a free land, the sidewalks thick with people waiting for loved ones. Strangers offered us bread and something to drink. I thanked them and knelt to pick up some of the soil of the free land and kiss it. Chuin Man, who had been so brave all during the tiring journey, began to cry. Ice cream, toys—nothing could comfort his little heart. It was as if he knew that, for the first time in his life, he was free to express himself.

"Thank You, God," I said, "for delivering us. Thank You that the land on which we stand is not enslaved but free. From this day on, Lord, give me the grace to lift up Jesus and tell people that what You have done in my life You can do also in theirs. I want to serve You with all my heart. In the name of Jesus."

We kept walking, searching the faces of the crowds to see if Kai Sing was there to meet us. Face after face, but no sign of him. Then I recognized his brother and sister-in-law from a picture I had seen. They could never have recognized me from a picture, because all my features were so swollen with fluid, but I walked over and told them who I was. It was almost impossible for them to understand me, because they spoke in Cantonese and I spoke in Mandarin, but they took me to a hotel where my mother-in-law had sent a servant to help me take care of my son. Kai Sing had been unable to meet me, they managed to convey, because he didn't have the right legal papers to make the trip.

We had to wait for a few days in Macao before arrangements were completed for new identification papers that would permit us to enter Hong Kong. While I waited I was afraid, exhausted, and sick, but I was also amazed to see all the gambling going on, with free food and drink for the gamblers. Since I had just come from a place where there was not enough food to go around, I could hardly believe my eyes. It was wonderful to have enough to eat—but I was sorry I could not communicate well with my brother-in-law and his wife. Feeling the old loneliness welling up inside me, I had to remind myself that the living God was with me and would never forsake me.

When Chuin Man and I got off the boat in Hong Kong, the police took over. I quaked with fear, but there were no problems after all. My father-in-law's money had made the way. All the legalities had been taken care of, and we were quickly approved for entry.

I was greeted by two or three carloads of relatives—my husband, his whole immediate family, and numerous other relatives. I was ashamed of how I looked, not just my enormous size—I knew they would excuse that because of my advanced pregnancy—but because I saw so much luxury around me. There were cars, and well-dressed, well-fed people. I had not been accustomed to seeing any of that for years and years.

I was rushed into one of the waiting cars and taken to the home of my in-laws. It was a beautiful three-story, old-fashioned Chinese house with two stone lions guarding the entrance to the front door. The ground-floor apartments were rented out to other families, I would live on the second floor, and my in-laws lived on the third. It was cool and comfortable inside, and there are no words to express how grateful I was that God had supplied me with an air-conditioned environment after the sweltering conditions in the labor camp and on our journey to freedom.

In Chinese tradition, it is customary for a new bride to serve tea to her husband's family at the wedding. Since Kai Sing's parents had been in Hong Kong when we were married in Shanghai, I had never performed this little ceremony. The first thing I did when I entered their home was to pour cups of tea and hand them to my in-laws. Then they gave me four bars of gold, worth twelve hundred Hong Kong dollars, and officially received me into the Lam family.

I wept when I was reunited with my precious daughter, Chuin Way. How she had grown, and how much she had learned since our tearful goodbyes in Canton months ago! I was not surprised to learn that she had become the darling of the household. And I held my breath when the nanny who had accompanied her recounted the harrowing details of her escape into Hong Kong. It looked as if the Lord was performing miracle after miracle for each member of our family who was getting out of Red China.

But I was heartbroken to see that living in freedom had not helped Kai Sing. He was still acting so strangely—he was almost insanely angry that I had left our money and other valuables in the safe-deposit box, leaving the key with my mother. Even after I explained to him that the Communists had required me to send my wedding ring back, he refused to understand that I would not have been permitted to bring anything of value with me.

A few days after my arrival in Hong Kong, my mother-in-law took me to see an obstetrician. I had a brief but expensive hospitalization with false labor pains. Then the doctor sent me home to wait for the real thing to begin.

Was something wrong with the baby? Was God going to make me carry this child inside me forever?

Two weeks later, on August 20, after a very difficult labor, I held a fat little son in my arms, and everyone was overjoyed. For a few hours, even Kai Sing seemed happy as his mother made phone calls to inform all our relatives and friends.

Twenty-four hours after I'd given birth, I broke out with a terrible rash all over my body. I supposed it was from being so exhausted. And it didn't help matters much to be thinking that as soon as I had recovered I would need to look for a job. Kai Sing's income was not adequate to support our family, and I couldn't stand the thought of being dependent on our in-laws to provide for us.

"Oh, God, show me what I'm supposed to do!" became my daily cry. And it was a cry from the depths of my heart.

My mother and I.

Here I am as
a university student
(above) and as a
bride *(right)*.

My daughter, Ruth. I had to send her away from Shanghai with her nanny when she was only a year old so she would not starve to death.

When Chuin Man was still a child I could carry in my arms, we watched the train pull out of the station, taking his father away from China. I didn't know whether we would ever see him again.

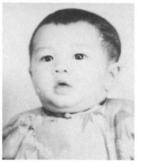

Joseph, my child of promise, the the son I carried in my womb for twelve months.

Our passport to freedom.

Hong Kong days.

Kathryn Kuhlman brought me
to America. Here we are
in Youngstown, Ohio.

I had a number of
different jobs in Las Vegas
in order to support my family.
At one time I worked as a
cook in the restaurant of
the Stardust Hotel.

The children were growing up when my mother and I moved them to San Jose from Las Vegas. I felt I needed to get them away from the gambling atmosphere.

My precious mother, "Grandma Sung," 1901–1979.

S. K. Sung and I on our wedding day.

My father's grave in Shanghai before the Communists seized the land and cremated his body. When my mother went to be with the Lord, we buried my father's ashes with her.

Left: Neng Yao was just a boy when I left China. *Below left:* After twenty years' separation, the thrilling sight of my brother and his precious wife and baby at the airport in Hong Kong. *Below right:* Mother, daughter, and son—reunited at long last.

Our family today (left to right):
Back row: Joe and his wife Sue, Ruth, Paul's wife Susie, Paul.
Standing: Gloria, Florence (called Wei Wei)
Seated: S. K. with Jackie on his lap, me with Julie on my lap

Preaching to the World Association of Christians against Communism in October 1978, I told them about the mighty power of the Holy Spirit, who can accomplish what man could never do.

Above: I signed a radio contract with Mr. Lee Shih Feng, Chairman of the Broadcasting Company of China. *Below:* General Wu greeted S. K. Sung and me with joy. He wanted to give his testimony about how Jesus had healed him.

Above: Signing the first TV contract with the president of CTV– to spread the gospel. *Top left:* Talking with newsmen in Taiwan. *Bottom left:* Here I am presenting a Bicentennial Bible to Yen Chia-Kan, president of the Republic of China, which recently awarded me a decoration for being such a good friend to my people there. *Below:* Pastors come from all over the free Republic of China to learn more about the work of the Holy Spirit, to help with Crusades, to seek counseling—and to pray.

10

"HE WILL BAPTIZE YOU . . ."

One crucial area in which I needed the Lord's guidance in my new life in Hong Kong was in the matter of which church to attend. I wanted to be in a place where I could grow as a Christian.

There were a lot of different denominational churches in Hong Kong, and people recommended first this one and then that one to me. I tried churches all over the city, but most of them seemed the same—dead as far as the power of God was concerned. I would go in and sit for a while and two songs would be sung and someone would read a prayer that had been written down on a piece of paper or printed in a book. The prayer always seemed rather meaningless to me. Then the announcements would be given about what night the choir would practice or when they would have a meeting about the budget. Someone would sing a solo and the minister would preach a sermon with three or four points which never seemed relevant to the problems I was facing in my life. And of course he never mentioned anything about the miracles God could do today or how we could call upon Him for help when everything was hopeless.

When an altar call was given, sometimes one or two

would come forward to transfer their membership from some other congregation where they couldn't get along with the minister or where they didn't like the choir director. But it was rare for anybody to come forward to receive the Lord. They all thought they had received Him already, but they didn't act like He was real to them. After we were dismissed with a prayer, we'd stretch and yawn and go home. Later we would come back for the next service, but again nothing would happen.

Looking around me, I felt that most of the people in the churches came to show off their furs or their beautiful clothes. And in the services, everything had to be just right—the altar cloths the right color and the right length, the flower arrangement just so, and the ushers with freshly pressed and cleaned suits and neckties that matched.

The presence of God seemed far away—but the people didn't notice. Somewhere, somehow, I thought, even in Hong Kong, there must be Christians who knew that God was real. I cried to the Lord to lead me to a place that was aware of Jesus and the power of His Spirit. I wasn't hungry to know more about dead religion—I was starving to experience more of the living God!

"Lord, show me the place where You want me to go!"

A few days after my anguished prayer, I saw a newspaper article about a meeting being held in a large stadium in the city. The article said that people were being healed at the meetings—goiters were disappearing, cancers were melting away, cripples were walking and leaping and praising God.

A stadium isn't a church, I reasoned. It's for sports events. Surely nobody would go there just to show off their fancy clothes and shake hands with each other. I decided to go to see for myself what was happening.

It was December 1958, and the weather was biting cold. I dressed warmly, putting on wool slacks and gloves. As I left the house, I prayed, "Jesus, I want to see Your power tonight. Please let me find more of You."

I had such a longing in my heart to know the deeper things of God, such a need to live above painful circumstances, such hungering to be in the abundant life God promised to His children.

What an experience it was for me to hear a message anointed by the Spirit of the living God! The evangelist proclaimed there *is* victory in Jesus, and that He can flood our lives and our beings with His presence and give us power and make us His witnesses in the world so that all men will come to know Him. He can heal our diseases, make the lame to walk, give sight to the blind, hearing to the deaf, cause us to leap for joy, and speak to us so we can hear Him! The evangelist said that all these things could be ours today, just as they were when Jesus walked as a man on the earth—because Jesus is still present among us by His Spirit.

How excited I was! That was exactly what my heart had been yearning to hear about—the real presence of God in my life every moment of every day.

At the first altar call, many went forward to receive Jesus as their Lord and Savior. Others went forward to receive healing at the hands of God. One woman with a huge goiter went forward, and as the people prayed for a miracle and laid hands on her, the goiter disappeared. I saw it with my own eyes!

Night after night I went to the meetings, and my faith was greatly strengthened. Every time the evangelist would say, "Every head bowed, and every eye closed," I would open my eyes wider than ever, so I could see everything that was going on. Although it seemed that I had suffered through a long lifetime already, I was only twenty-six, and I wanted to know for certain if miracles were really happening or if someone was only trying to fool the people.

When a man claimed he had been healed of a tumor, I sought him out and asked, "Is it really true?" He smiled and said yes. Later he showed me a letter from his doctor and X-rays that confirmed his healing.

When a woman got up from a wheelchair and walked, I went over to her and asked, "Were you really crippled before?"

She laughed and cried, "Oh yes! I've been in the wheelchair for twenty years, unable to walk at all. And now look at me!" She was striding back and forth as if she could have climbed a mountain.

And people whose blind eyes had been opened confirmed their healings too:

"Yes, praise God! I was blind, but now I can see!"

If I had been understanding my Bible, I would not have been surprised at the things I was seeing, because Jesus said that such signs would follow those who believed, but at that time I was terribly ignorant of the promises in God's Word. I had been filled with doubt because I had never been taught the full gospel. But in the meetings, He was gradually bringing me closer and closer to a fullness of faith, growing me up to the place where I would really *know* that nothing is impossible for God.

After the evangelistic meetings in the stadium were over, a Christian center was begun in downtown Hong Kong to carry on the work of the ministry. I had been asked to serve as an usher during the stadium crusade, finding people their seats and handing out song sheets. Then I was hired to work as a secretary for the Christian center and to help out in other ways—waxing the floors, scrubbing the toilets, doing anything that needed to be done. I was glad to help in any way I could. And every day I saw more people saved and healed by the power of God.

One Wednesday night at the close of a prayer meeting, a special invitation was given for those who wanted to receive the Baptism with the Holy Spirit that Jesus promised to all who really believed in Him. I was ready to receive this empowering gift of God for my own life, so I went forward to the altar. I didn't want to continue to live as half a Christian—I wanted to receive all His blessing, everything He had for me.

The pastor's wife instructed me in the steps I was to follow: I was to confess my sin and yield everything in my life to God. Then I was to ask Jesus to baptize me in His Holy Spirit.

As I followed her instructions, I felt an amazing and totally unexpected thing happen. All the fear and hatred that had been in me toward my grandmother and my cousins and the Japanese and the Communists drained out of me. In their place, I was overwhelmed with the love of Jesus for all those who had persecuted and abused me. My heart longed for all of them to know Jesus as I knew Him at that moment.

As I looked heavenward, I was covered with the indescribable joy of His presence. And when I opened my mouth, the Spirit of God began praising the Lord through my lips in a heavenly language I had never learned. I could have listened to it forever.

My spirit had been set free so I could really worship Him! And I would never be the same again.

11

"GIVE AND IT SHALL BE GIVEN"

Perfection didn't set in overnight, of course, but the Lord was with me in a powerful new way, and He began to teach me more about how to trust Him in everything. The lessons weren't always easy. For instance, in the matter of money . . .

I really loved to hear the preaching, and I loved to sing the wonderful songs of praise with the rest of the congregation. The praying was beautiful—it really touched my heart. Everything about every service was always filled with blessing for me—I was cheerful about all of it—until the preacher got to the part where he talked about how the Lord loves a cheerful giver. That bothered me. It really turned me off.

I wasn't cheerful about giving, because I figured I didn't have anything to give. Although Kai Sing was working,. his pay was so small that I felt a heavy responsibility to help feed and clothe us all, and my salary at the Christian center was only one hundred fifty dollars a month. When the offering basket was passed, I would always pretend to be inspecting my fingernails, reading my Bible, or doing something else, just so I would have an excuse not to put anything in the basket. I hoped no one would notice, but I was noticing all right. So was the Lord.

I was apologizing to Him about it one night in January at a special service where the missionaries were talking about the desperate need for funds to pay the bills from the big meetings and to continue the outreach program to the unsaved people in Hong Kong. It had cost a lot of money to rent the stadium and to pay for all the literature they had been handing out for over three weeks. I hadn't given a penny.

"Lord, You surely understand why I can't be cheerful when they start talking about all this giving. It makes me uncomfortable, because I don't have anything to give. If it weren't for my mother-in-law's help, we'd all be starving. Remember, Lord, I'm a refugee. I came out of China as a beggar, bringing nothing with me, not even my wedding ring."

But the Lord didn't understand that I had nothing to give. In fact, He reminded me I had four bars of gold in a safe-deposit box right there in Hong Kong, the gold bars my mother-in-law had given me when I had served her that first cup of tea in her house. The gold was worth about twelve hundred dollars, I knew, but I hadn't realized the Lord knew about my safe-deposit box. I had been careful to keep that a secret from everybody.

For a minute, I wondered how He had found out about it, and where I could hide the gold so He couldn't see it, but then I remembered that God sees everything, everywhere, all the time.

I almost cried when He told me to give the four bars of gold to Him by putting them in the offering basket. Maybe I could explain to Him how it was:

"You don't understand, Lord. Those gold bars are my emergency fund. If anything should happen to me so I can't work, I'll need to sell them so I can feed my kids. They're all I have. If I give them to You, I'll have nothing.

"You understand now, don't You, Lord?"

I didn't hear Him say okay, so I knew He hadn't

changed His mind. But being a lawyer, and not wanting to get emotional and go overboard, I persuaded myself that maybe He would settle for fifty-fifty.

The next day I went to the bank, got out two of the gold bars, and when the offering basket was passed that night, dropped them in it. I was hoping everyone would see me because I was giving so much—half of all I had in the world.

But afterward, instead of feeling good about it, I felt guilty. I didn't receive a blessing from the giving at all. What was wrong? Wasn't that good enough for Him? It was more than anyone else had given, I was certain. And surely He knew I needed to save *something* for emergency use.

He was asking too much.

That night, I couldn't sleep. I tossed and turned until morning, because I was so miserable inside. Before I got up for the day, God spoke to me:

"My daughter," His voice was so gentle, not condemning at all, "haven't I proved to you time and time again that I am able to supply all your needs—even for the things that money can't buy? Don't you know that you don't need any emergency fund when you have Me?"

Oh, I felt so ashamed. I thought of the day when I had stood before the firing squad and He had performed a miracle of deliverance for me. I thought of how He had saved me from the lethal Japanese bombs, from dying on the mountain of coal, and how He had kept my unborn children from harm when I was carrying them in my womb . . .

All the gold bars in the world could not have taken care of those emergencies for me. Only God. And here I was, rebelling, wanting to hold back two powerless bars of gold from Jesus. *"Rebellion is as the sin of witchcraft,"* I remembered from His Word. And I knew then that if I didn't give everything to the Lord, I would be cutting myself off from His blessing. I would be saying that I didn't trust Him with my whole heart, that I didn't love Him, that I didn't believe His love for me.

"Oh, Lord, forgive me, forgive me, forgive me!"

I hurried to the bank as soon as it opened and told the attendant, "You may give me the two-dollar refund for the key to my safe-deposit box, because I won't be needing it anymore."

That night, the minister quoted the scripture from Malachi 3:10:

> Bring ye all the tithes into the storehouse, that there may be meat in mine house, and prove me now herewith, saith the Lord of hosts, if I will not open you the windows of heaven, and pour you out a blessing, that there shall not be room enough to receive it.

In those words, Jesus was saying to me, "My daughter, I don't need your money. I own all that is. But you need My blessing—the blessing you cannot receive unless you give your all to Me. What you give to Me, I will give back to you—abundantly, pressed down, heaped up, running together, spilling over."

I could hardly wait for the offering basket to reach me. And when I laid my last two bars of gold in it, I wanted to jump in the basket myself and say, "Lord, here I am. I am giving my whole life to You."

12

TO SET THE CAPTIVES FREE

I was beginning to enjoy all the benefits of being a new creature in Christ Jesus, filled with His Spirit, living in a land of freedom. But my mother and my brother—and my father's body—were still locked behind the Bamboo Curtain. They had no hope of release except for my faith in God's promise that we would all be delivered. But how could it be accomplished?

I felt that my brother was safe for the time being, but I knew my mother was beginning to be questioned and persecuted already. I didn't write to her often, and I had to be very guarded in what I said, because it could be dangerous for her if someone intercepted a letter critical of the government. But I prayed often and longed to know how she could be rescued from the hard persecution that was sure to come.

The Communists had ways of finding out everything about everyone, sooner or later, and I figured they already knew that she, like my father, had come from a very wealthy background. Her father had been one of China's wealthiest merchants, one of the leading traders of seafood with Japan. He had had two wives, a common practice in those days, and he had given the Hung Ying Library, one of Shanghai's largest, to the country. Growing up in a rich neighborhood, mother had been a friend of the girl who later became Madame Chiang Kai-shek. She had been well educated in Chinese and American schools, becoming what was called a "social Christian" in the missionary school. "Social Christians" were people who said they would accept Jesus, but they didn't really know the Lord or believe in Him. They just took the step of affirmation because it was convenient, and to please the missionaries.

A tiny woman, not even five feet tall, my mother had never known what it was to work. Like other women in her social circle, she had spent her days in private and social clubs, often playing bridge, poker, and mahjong for many hours a day. But during the war with Japan, she had laid down her former lifestyle to go into the con-centration camps with my father to minister to the needs of the American prisoners there—taking their clothes home to wash, giving them medicine, dressing their wounds, and showing love for them in any way she could.

The Communists would be sure to persecute her for all these things.

One night as I was praying for her safety, I said, "Dear Lord, you know how much I love my little mother, and how much I want her to know You as I know You. How can I help her?"

That night, He spoke to my heart and repeated His promise that my whole family would get out of Red China. I wanted to believe it was possible for my mother, but I knew how impossible it was. Humanly speaking, there was no argument I could think of that would persuade the authorities to give her a permit to leave the country. Besides, she had been so weak with heart trouble she hadn't even been able to take a bath by herself for many months. As I recalled the hardships of my own journey to freedom, I knew there was no way she could make it. The walk across no man's land in itself would kill her.

But I had prayed, and God had a plan. I was learning that He always has a plan, and that my job is to fit into it.

On January 4, 1960, I went with our church youth group to Aberdeen, a fishing village where people lived on sampans in the harbor. We passed out tracts and Oral Roberts's literature, and witnessed to the sampan dwellers. Oh, how they needed to know the Lord! They existed in such awful squalor, several generations spending their lives crowded together on the little fishing boats with their strange sails, with no hope of anything better. The filthy water of the harbor where they caught enough tiny fish to eke out a wretched existence was like an open sewer.

We had finished handing out our literature, and had led several people to the Lord and were ready to go home. I was walking on the edge of the wharf when someone accidentally bumped into me, knocking me from the weathered wood of the pier to the harbor twenty feet below. The tide was out, so I landed halfway in the vile water and halfway on a large pile of rocks resting in the slick mud of the harbor bottom.

When I regained consciousness, I was lying on clean white sheets. There was a plaster cast on my left ankle, a sizeable knot on my head, and I ached all over. A nurse told me that I had been brought in by ambulance, that my ankle was broken, and that it would be a long time before I could expect to walk again.

When relatives came to see me, they couldn't resist making fun of me:

"You were working for your 'living God,' Neng Yee. Why would He let something like this happen to you? Why didn't He hold you up with His right arm?" They almost collapsed with derisive laughter; then one of them rubbed it in a little harder:

"If it's so good to serve the Lord, Neng Yee, why did He let you fall into that stinking harbor and nearly kill yourself?"

I had no answer that would satisfy them, but I was satisfied myself that God was going to use the situation for good for me somehow, because His Word promised that He was working all things for good for the ones who loved Him and were called to do His work. I knew that I was one of them, all right, and that He would vindicate Himself if I would continue to trust in Him.

As I lay in bed day after day, I praised the Lord, waiting for the good I knew would come from my fall into the sea at Aberdeen.

During my long recuperation, I had two special communications from the Lord. The first came one night as I lay in bed praying that God would find some way to use me for His glory. With my eyes closed, suddenly I saw myself standing before an audience of thousands of green-eyed and blue-eyed people. I was talking to them about Jesus.

I must be dreaming, I told myself at first. Then, *But I'm not asleep! But this couldn't be a vision from God, because those aren't my people. He could never use me with people like that!*

Having registered my protest, I put it from my mind.

The next special communication came one morning about ten o'clock. As I was lying in bed, a breeze came in the window and blew the curtains gently back and forth. I heard the voice of God clearly say to me, "Neng Yee, now is the time for your mother to come out of Red China. She will be with you soon."

I knew the Lord would do His part in making the impossible thing come to pass, but there was a part for me to do too. But how could I do anything? I was too helpless to go anywhere.

Immediately the Lord brought to my mind Yee Ah Hsing, the nanny who had brought my daughter out of

Red China. She was very strong; I had known her to carry loads weighing a hundred pounds or more and still walk very fast. So I summoned her and asked if she could carry me down the stairs. That was no problem for her. Very soon after the birth of my third child, ninety pounds of excess weight had fallen from me, so I was no longer too big to be carried.

After I was downstairs, I called a cab and went to the emergency room of the Queen Mary Hospital where I had been treated after my fall into the harbor. I got from them a written report of my accident and copies of the X-rays showing my broken ankle. When I returned home, I scissored accounts of my accident from the newspapers and sent all this information to my mother for her to submit to the authorities so they would release her to come to Hong Kong and help me with my babies during my convalescence.

Six weeks later, I hadn't heard a thing, and it was time for my cast to be removed. New X-rays were taken, and when the doctor had examined them, he shook his head in despair.

"I'm very sorry we were in such a hurry at the time of your accident. The bone was set incorrectly, and now it must be rebroken and set again."

"Jesus, why? Why?" I went home and wept for a long time.

"Neng Yee, have I ever failed you? Have I ever forsaken you? Haven't I promised you that *all* things are working out for good?"

"Yes, Lord, but I can't see the good in having my leg broken again and having to lie here another six weeks. I see only misery and pain, and people continuing to laugh at me and make fun of You, saying I serve a weak God. What can You possibly accomplish in this? I'm afraid I don't understand."

When relatives heard the news that I would have to

have my leg rebroken, they came to point their fingers at me again and ridicule me for trusting in a God who would let such a thing happen to me. It was just as I had feared. Then I really got down to business with Him:

"You see, Lord? *Now* what do You want me to do?"

"Have the operation and send a new set of reports to your mother. She didn't take the first set to the authorities; she thought you were making up the whole thing, because you were longing for her to get out. But these will persuade her—and them."

The second operation took place in March, and a fat bundle of certified documents was sent to my mother. The cast came off in May, and I was able to get up, but the pain when I finally stood on my own two feet was like walking on thousands of needles. I was *so* discouraged.

One day the pastor from my church came and brought me a pair of crutches to use. And he offered to send a car for me so I could go back to work without having to stand on a crowded streetcar. While he was talking with me, I told him about my mother behind the Bamboo Curtain and asked the church to join me in praying daily for her release.

When I was in the doctor's office one afternoon for therapy, I told the nurse about my mother's need to get out of Red China and the problems we were having in securing her release. She was so touched that, although in the past I had to wait four or five hours before my turn at therapy, I never had to wait again. And the doctor said that all the treatments he had given me, treatments that would have cost around eight hundred dollars, would not cost me a penny.

Yes, God was working some things for good for me. But May passed, and June, July, August—and still no word from the Mainland. Sometimes I would wonder if my mother was still alive. But then I would remember God's promise.

"Why, God? Why are You being so slow? You told me long ago that my mother would be freed. I still believe it, but everyone else thinks I'm a fool."

The one who thought I was the greatest fool of all was Kai Sing. Ever since I had come to Hong Kong, he had been angry all the time. Sometimes he would literally kick me out of bed at night—even when I had the plaster cast on my leg. And when I was disabled, he never offered to help me with anything.

"Let your precious church help you!" he raged.

Sometimes he would take my paycheck away from me and then beat me for not having any money to give him. I couldn't understand any of it, and I felt so sorry for myself.

First I had suffered under the Japanese, then under my awful grandmother, then under the Communists. Now, when all that was behind me and I was in a free land, my husband was treating me like an enemy. Because our children were small and I knew they needed a mother *and* a father, I felt helpless to do anything about it, even when the physical abuse he inflicted on me was too sadistic to be believed.

Of course I dared not tell anyone. The whole family would lose face if it became known that my husband was abusing me. I had no one to turn to but the Lord, and in it all I drew closer and closer to Him.

One night when the church was in the midst of a revival, I arrived home about ten o'clock, too tired to undress and go to bed. Instead, I just threw myself, fully clothed, across the couch and fell asleep.

Soon I was being awakened by a very young-looking woman in a shining robe.

"Neng Yee, Neng Yee, wake up, wake up!" she said. "I'm an angel, sent to you by the Lord. He has heard your prayers, and has sent me to deliver a message to you. Your mother will be coming out of Red China tomorrow. Get everything ready."

With that, she was gone. The door of the room was locked as it had been. There was no way for a "person" to have come in or out—my visitor with the wonderful news *had* to be a spiritual being of some kind.

I was so excited I could hardly contain myself. It was three o'clock in the morning, but I woke up my husband, the children, the maid, the neighbors, and everybody, telling them that God had spoken to me through an angel and that my mother was getting out from Red China the next day. I got on the elevator and went up and down on every floor, shouting the good news. Everyone scolded me for disturbing their rest, called me a crazy woman, and tried to go back to sleep, but I was too excited to sleep. I got on the telephone and called all of my girlfriends in town so they could rejoice with me.

The next morning, I went to a friend and borrowed a hundred dollars to buy furniture for my mother and to rent a room for her. Then I went to work as usual. That night, the evangelistic meeting lasted until very late, and it was nearly midnight when I reached home. To my surprise, no one had gone to bed. *Something must be wrong*, I thought. Everyone was standing and staring at me, as if I had come from outer space. Then their eyes moved in the direction of a piece of paper lying on the table.

It was a telegram from my mother, from whom I had not heard in months and months.

"I am on my way to you, Neng Yee," the telegram said. And it was signed, "Mother." The telegram had been sent from Macao, only forty miles from Hong Kong. My mother had come out of Red China that very day, just as God had said she would!

A moment later I heard something crash to the floor in the kitchen, and I ran to see what had happened. There stood Yee Ah Hsing, who had brought my daughter out of China and who had carried me down the stairs so I could go to the hospital and get the X-rays. And on the floor, smashed deliberately into a million pieces where she had hurled it, was what had been a statue of Buddha.

"Oh, mistress," she cried. "I have served Buddha all my life. I didn't trust your Lord; I just thought you had gone crazy to believe in something you couldn't see. But last night you told us what He had said to you, and today you received the telegram saying it's true. Today I want to know your God. I want your Jesus to be my Jesus."

We were both weeping as I led her in a sinner's prayer of confession and repentance, and when I laid my hands on her, the Holy Spirit fell upon her and suffused her being. Yee Ah Hsing broke out speaking her overflowing joy in a heavenly language she had never learned.

The next day I went to Macao to get my mother. When she saw me coming, she got up and walked toward me. We got closer and closer and finally we were holding each other in our arms.

"Mother, you have arrived in a free land!"

"Yes, Neng Yee. I didn't know where I would get the strength for such a hard journey, but when my exit permit was ready, the power came down from somewhere. And miracles, too. It was raining, but the moment I stepped from the house to get in the car, the rain stopped until I was in its shelter. Your trust in Jesus must have had something to do with my escape.

"Neng Yee, it is because of your faith that I am here today. Once I didn't believe your faith, but now I understand it is true. Our God is real. He alone is the living God."

My cup overflowed.

13

HELP OF THE HELPLESS

After my mother's release from Red China, I needed a job that paid more money, since now I had the added responsibility of feeding and clothing her. So I resigned my position after working at the Christian center for two years.

Almost immediately I got a job as a schoolteacher. That was a miracle in itself, because ordinarily the British government of Hong Kong would not honor teaching credentials from Mainland China, but in my case they made an exception. And what a blessing it was for me to work with the little fifth-grade children each day. But the income was still inadequate.

When I saw an advertisement in the newspaper for a social worker in the city of Hong Kong, I thought the job would hold tremendous opportunities for me to witness to refugees and help them in a material way as well. But there were obstacles to be overcome. My English was so bad that it would be very difficult for me to pass the required examination for the position. I thought also of all the reports a social worker would be required to compile every day, and I knew it would be impossible for me to qualify for the job.

"But God can do impossible things," I reminded

myself, "and if He wants me to have the position, He will arrange it."

When I went to the office to fill out an application for the job, I learned that many other persons were seeking it because the salary was so attractive—$560 in Hong Kong dollars a month. I had been getting only $150 a month at the Christian Center, and my teaching salary was a meager $350 a month.

When I found out there would be two examinations for the position, one written and one oral, my faith was put to another test. How could I even begin to pass a written test, with my English ability so limited? And the oral examination—how could anyone understand my answers?

"But if I don't step into the Red Sea, it will never part," I insisted to myself. "Lord, I'm going to take the test, and You must help me."

For three days, I studied night and day, poring over books about Hong Kong. Soon I had memorized important details—size, population, and many things about the people. As I studied, the Lord seemed to impress on me the importance of learning certain additional facts, as if they were the ones I would be required to know to pass the examination.

When the day came for me to take the written test, I had never felt more inadequate. A friend of mine, who had graduated from St. John's University in Shanghai and had been living in Hong Kong for three years, working for the telephone company, was among the people in the waiting room, but I was too frightened to visit with her. I knew that many of the applicants were graduates of Hong Kong University. They looked so elegant, and conversed so fluently in perfect English, that I knew I didn't have a chance. It was only natural that the authorities would prefer to hire students from their own university, and I decided to back out and not take the examination after all.

But suddenly my name was called. It was too late to leave.

I was asked how long I had been in Hong Kong and where I had received my schooling. I understood the questions, but I wasn't sure the examiner understood my frightened answers. After the initial screening, I sat in a corner, dreading what was to come next. The test was to last for three hours, and we were not permitted to talk or to ask any questions of the examiners.

But no one said I couldn't talk to God. I would need all the help He could give me. When I was handed the test papers, I prayed, "Lord, I understand that, in the old days, the Spirit spoke to the prophets and wrote the Bible through them. If You want me to work in this Social Welfare Department, You're going to have to give me the words to write. Help me remember all I have studied. Thank You, Jesus."

I picked up my pen and started to write.

The first question dealt with the reasons I wanted to work with the Social Welfare Department. Because my heart was overflowing with compassion for the refugees, it was easy for me to answer that one. The second question involved a case study of a sampan family. With what eager interest I had studied the material about them, knowing some of it already from my church contacts with the fisherfolk before I fell into the harbor.

After about fifty minutes, I had written everything I could. Everyone else was still working away, but I saw no reason just to sit there after I had written all I knew, so I handed in my test and went home.

"No one else left before the three hours were up," my girlfriend said when she telephoned later in the day. "Maybe you left something out."

My heart sunk to my shoetops, but the Lord wouldn't let me feel sorry for myself.

"Neng Yee, I told you what to write and you wrote it.

That was all you could do. Anything else would have been a waste of time."

A few weeks later I was called for a second interview by the chief of the Child Welfare Section of the Department. She told me she was a Roman Catholic and that the Lord had prompted her to interview me instead of one of the others. When the interview was finished, she told me to get a character reference from a minister and have a physical examination.

I got the job!

As a worker in the Child Welfare Department, I was privileged to call on the children of hundreds of destitute families. It was wonderful to be able to help them with food and clothing. It was even more wonderful to tell them about the living Lord Jesus who could meet all their needs. God was so good!

It was soon apparent that my mother had gotten out of Red China just in time. By 1961 there were frantic hordes trying to get across the border to escape the awful persecution by the Communists. They were climbing over the mountains, swimming across the rivers, being smuggled in the holds of tiny boats—coming in every conceivable way, all of them dangerous, in a desperate effort to reach freedom. Many died during the attempt to escape. Some of those who survived fared little better, roaming the streets like packs of wild dogs—thirsty, hungry, weary, with nowhere to go.

Many police and other government workers were sent to the border to try to keep order. Refugee centers had been set up by the British government, but it was impossible to handle all the refugees because of their great numbers. There just wasn't enough space, food, water, or clothing for such a horde. Sanitation was inadequate, disease was rampant, and the labor market was glutted. The authorities began to face the awful fact that to admit any more refugees to Hong Kong would be to increase the sickness and death among those who had made it to freedom. Inevitably, the day came when barriers were erected to stop the flow of refugees. They were no longer permitted to come into Hong Kong. Furthermore, people living in Hong Kong were forbidden to give aid, comfort, or support to persons crossing the border.

I was heartsick seeing and hearing about the misery of so many people and being prohibited from helping them through my job. Would the ravages of Communism on the human race ever end?

During this time, Kai Sing was becoming increasingly cruel to me. I didn't dare mention it to anyone, but carried the hideous burden locked up inside myself. Finally I decided that if I stopped work entirely and spent all my time waiting on him, showing him love, making him feel secure, he might recover from the effects of persecution and we could have a happy family once more.

But it didn't work.

The first week after I resigned from my job, my mother wasn't feeling well and I needed to call a doctor to come to see her. Since I didn't have any money to pay him, I borrowed fifty dollars from my maid. After the doctor left, Kai Sing came home and said he had lost a hundred dollars from his pocket. Then he accused me of stealing it to pay the doctor. He went into such a rage that he slapped my face and kicked me in the chest with his shoes on until I ran to the bathroom and vomited blood.

I was so upset that for the first time I telephoned Kai Sing's mother and reported his actions to her, thinking she might know some way I could help him. But she refused to believe me. Instead of suggesting some way to help her son, she told me I must be crazy.

The malicious cruelty continued and grew unimaginably worse. I visited a psychiatrist to see if he could help, but he had no answers. Finally I came to the place where I wanted to die rather than to continue living in such torment.

Determined to take my life, I went to the rooftop of the thirteen-story apartment building where we were living and walked over to the waist-high parapet around the edge of the roof. There I leaned over and looked down on the bustling street below. If I jumped, death would be certain, easy, and quick. I started to climb onto the narrow ledge from which I could throw myself down and be finished forever with all the agony of living.

In the split second before I could make my leap to destruction, I felt a little hand tugging at my shoe, and a frightened little voice saying, "Mama, mama, I need you."

Unknown to me, little Chuin Man had followed me up the stairs to the roof. He was God's instrument for saving my life, and returning me to sanity.

Of *course* he needed me. All the children did. And my mother too. What could I have been thinking of! Even Kai Sing needed me!

I fell from the parapet back onto the graveled rooftop and lay there weeping, while my son squatted beside me and patted my hair to comfort me.

"God, forgive me! Forgive me, Lord." Restored to reality, I knew I could *never* kill myself. My life didn't belong to me, it belonged to God. And He had work for me to do in caring for my mother, in loving my children. And I couldn't let Kai Sing kill me either, or continue to torture me. No one had that right.

The next day I was in the church office and the pastor was asking me, as he had asked me many times before, why my arm was bruised, why I had a black eye, why there was such a large burn on my leg. I still couldn't permit myself to tell him, but suddenly the Holy Spirit supernaturally revealed the answer to him. His eyebrows went up in surprise.

"Oh!" he exclaimed. "It is your husband who is torturing you!"

There was no need for me to deny it any longer. The Lord had shown the truth to him. It broke my heart to do it, but I nodded my head yes. And then I wept.

For a Chinese woman, it was like the end of the world.

14

AMERICA

Realizing that my life was in danger, the pastor of the church insisted that I leave my husband. But he was drinking heavily at the time, and I knew that if I left him, he would really kill me, as he had threatened to do many times. The only way I would be safe was to get out of the country. But how would I leave—and where would I go?

As I prayed and sought the Lord's will about all this, He brought the name of Kathryn Kuhlman so strongly to my mind that I began to believe that through her the Lord would open a door for me to find a new life.

I had been introduced to Miss Kuhlman when she had come to Hong Kong a few years earlier for some meetings. Later, someone had told her about my escape from Red China and my giving the four bars of gold to the missionaries. She loved stories like that, and she wanted me to come to the United States to give my testimony. Maybe she would even send me to Bible school, she said. Soon it was all arranged and I was on my way across the ocean.

I had never dared to believe that I would come to America, even after the vision God had given me in 1960 of speaking before a blue-eyed, green-eyed audience. That was beyond anything I could imagine. In the nine years I had been living in Hong Kong, being active in the church, I had never spoken before a group. Sometimes, when I had enough money, I had invited people to my home for a meal and then taken them with me to church services, but all my "witnessing" had been on a one-to-one basis. And of course I wouldn't have dared to give my testimony in Hong Kong about how God got me out of Red China. Hong Kong was too close to the Mainland for that; besides, Hong Kong itself was filled with Communists. There was no telling what they might do to me, so I had kept quiet.

As soon as I arrived on the West Coast of the United States, an American minister I had met in Hong Kong asked me to speak at his church. I agreed to do it, but since my English was very poor, I naturally expected him to have an interpreter for me. At the last moment, I found out there would be no interpreter. I would have to speak in English. I panicked.

"Lord, what am I going to do?"

"It's not what *you* are going to do—it's what *I* am going to do through you. Just yield yourself to Me, and I will speak to the people."

I got up in the pulpit, my knees shaking, and I poured out my heart. I could tell the people were moved by the Spirit as I spoke, whether or not they understood a word of what I said. God *had* done something in spite of my inadequacy.

The next thing I knew, I was in Pittsburgh getting on a bus to go to Miss Kuhlman's big meeting in Youngstown, Ohio. There were literally hundrds of buses going to the meeting, all of them full of people praising the Lord, and I wondered what I was getting into.

When we arrived at the big auditorium, one of Miss Kuhlman's helpers found me and said I was to come up front to tell my life story. And suddenly I was standing at a microphone in front of eight thousand people. To get me started, Miss Kuhlman asked me what I liked best about America so far, and I told the truth:

"MacDonald's hamburgers and Kentucky fried chicken."

Everybody laughed so hard, I could see they wanted to be my friends. I looked out at all those smiling faces and started to speak with tears in my eyes.

"Just before he died, my father told me to come to you blue-eyed, green-eyed black and white people, and I have finally found you. Your American missionaries told me about Jesus, so we are not strangers. I'm your sister, and you are my brothers and sisters. I never cried in front of my enemy, but I am crying in front of you, because you will love me and you will remember my tears and my people in your hearts."

Miss Kuhlman said, "Yes, honey, we are your American family," and all the people stood up and clapped their hands for at least five minutes. When they sat down, I knew I could talk to them from the bottom of my heart. It took nearly two hours for me to tell them all God had done for me, and when I finished, Miss Kuhlman stood up and cried and put her arm around me.

"The calling of God is on you, beloved," she said, "the great anointing of His Holy Spirit. Your story should be told all over the world."

I couldn't understand what she was talking about, but she was being kind to me and I adored her. Miss Kuhlman took me under her wing, and for weeks I traveled with her, ate with her, and carried the basket that held her Bible. She taught me American office procedures, and I thought she was a genius.

Miss Kuhlman introduced me to all her friends in restaurants and department stores and to the policemen who handled the traffic at her meetings, just as if I had been her child. She had me tell my story about the gold bars many times.

After forty-six days, when I had decided that Miss Kuhlman was my answer for everything and that I would be happy spending the rest of my life following her around, the Lord said, "No, Nora." (Sometimes He called me by the American name my mother had given me.) "It's time for you to move on. I haven't brought you here to be part of Miss Kuhlman's ministry forever. I have prepared you for a ministry of your own."

It was hard for me to leave Miss Kuhlman, especially when I didn't know where I would go or what I would do, but I picked up my suitcase and walked out.

For a while, I stayed in San Diego with an American housewife I had met at the church where I had given my first testimony. She told me an amazing thing.

When I spoke in her church, many of the people had complained that I talked so rapidly and with such poor English that they couldn't understand a word I was saying. And I had sounded so bitterly anti-Communist that I had almost made them sympathize with my enemies! But the most wicked man in town—someone who had never been in church before—had attended the meeting out of curiosity to hear the Chinese woman who said she had escaped from Communist China. And the power of God was so strong that he had been convicted of his sin of unbelief and had come back two weeks later to give his life to the Lord.

That really encouraged me that maybe I was to have a ministry in America after all, but I was so lonesome for my children that I could hardly stand it. The ministry would have to wait while I went back to Hong Kong in September of 1966 to bring them and even Kai Sing to the United States with me. Although he had threatened to kill me many times, I thought the United States was so different from China and Hong Kong and so far away from all memories of the Communist persecution that maybe Kai Sing could get hold of himself and start to be a good husband. I was more than willing to forgive him, to turn the other cheek and give our marriage one more chance.

It was a bad mistake. Kai Sing abused me more than ever, with more mental and physical torture than anyone could endure. And from the time he arrived in America, he never stopped threatening to kill me.

Oh, how I prayed the Lord would show me what to do next!

I was reduced to skin and bones, a nervous wreck. A lawyer advised me that if I did not leave my husband at once, soon my children would be without a mother. And I received confirmation from the Lord that he was right.

Leaving Kai Sing for good was the hardest decision of my life. What I had suffered in Red China seemed hardly worth mentioning compared with the way I hurt when I left him. Without telling him where I was going or what I was doing, I took the children out of school in Oakland one day in February 1967. An American missionary had given them American names by this time. Paul (Chuin Man) was eleven, Ruth (Chuin Way) was ten, and Joseph (Chuin Mo) was eight and a half. Looking at my beautiful, innocent children, I knelt down in the airport and cried to the Lord:

"What have I done wrong? Why do these children have to suffer so much? I don't know where to turn, Lord. I have only You."

He led us to Denver first, where we stayed for a few weeks with an American couple I had met in Hong Kong in 1958. When my lawyer notified me that my husband had refused to contribute to the support of our children, I did the unthinkable thing—I went to Las Vegas to establish my residence so I could file for divorce.

The divorce proceedings were an unspeakable nightmare. But the matter was finally settled, and I was awarded full custody of the children.

As a divorced woman, I knew no one would want me in the pulpit. I supposed I would go back to law school again, to get a degree that would be recognized outside of Red China so I could make a living practicing law. But God had other plans.

For several years after the divorce, I stayed on in Las Vegas, working at whatever job I could find—as a cook in the Stardust Hotel, an accounting clerk in a pawnshop, a teacher's aide in public school, a grocery store clerk. I even worked in a bank, unlocking a door to let people go to their safe-deposit boxes.

Then, to my surprise, the doors of many churches began to open for me to speak. When pastors heard my story, they were excited at what God had done. It seemed that everyone in America wanted to hear me. Sometimes I would find myself speaking four times on a single day on the weekend, crying my heart out every time. I didn't like telling my story, because there was too much suffering in it, and I had to live through all the pain again each time I told it. But I saw that the people were moved when I spoke, and I knew America needed to be warned of the evils of Communism before it was too late.

When I began to speak every weekend, I wired my mother to come to stay with me and help me take care of the children. For five years, I traveled from city to city, from church to church. And the more I spoke, the more I felt His anointing upon me.

15

PREPARING THE WAY

Things seemed to have settled down in my life at last. I was working as a teacher's aide during the week and flying to churches here and there to preach the gospel on the weekends. I had a good nanny to take care of the children, my precious mother was happy living with us, and time was healing the nightmare of the divorce proceedings. We were all part of the fellowship of a wonderful church . . .

But the feeling of being settled didn't last long. One day in 1971, the Lord told me I was to go to Taiwan, the free Republic of China, to preach the gospel to my own people there. Besides the native Taiwanese, there were on the island many Chinese who had fled the Mainland before and after the Communist takeover.

God's voice was so strong that I couldn't ignore it. But I didn't want to go.

"Lord, I don't have any desire to go back to China now. I don't want to minister there."

"Nora, I didn't bring you to America just so you could be welcomed and loved by the blue-eyed, green-eyed people. I didn't bring you here just so you could enjoy the sunshine and hamburgers and fried chicken. I brought you here to teach you the things you would need to know to minister to your own people."

"But Lord, I'm afraid to go to Taiwan. Besides, I don't have a single friend there. The seventeen million people are all strangers to me. Nobody would ask me to speak. They would never listen to a woman preacher. It would be a total waste of time for me to go there."

When I had finished my argument, He told me again that I was to go, but He didn't say exactly when, so I thought I would let the whole matter rest and maybe He would forget about it.

But that was not to be. Soon after He had spoken, someone mentioned my name in a meeting where a man named Jim Gerrard was in the congregation. Gerrard had never heard of me before, but as soon as he heard my name, the Spirit of the Lord fell upon him and he said, "The Lord has a prophecy for Nora Lam."

Jim Gerrard was widely known in the circles of the Full Gospel Businessmen's Fellowship International as a true prophet of God. When he said a thing would happen, it always happened. Later, he flew to Las Vegas so he could deliver God's message to me in person. When he stepped off the plane about five o'clock on that unforgettable afternoon, I thought I had never seen anyone so tall and thin—or with such a strange, other-worldly appearance.

"God has a message for you, Nora Lam," he said.

I almost covered my ears to keep from hearing it, because I knew I would have to do what he said, whether I liked it or not. I had no desire to be a missionary or an evangelist overseas, and I was afraid he was going to tell me to do that. But Jim Gerrard didn't care what I wanted. A prophet of God has to be faithful to the Lord's calling on his own life, and so he prophesied anyway, leaving nothing out.

The prophecy was far worse than I expected:

"Nora Lam," he said, "the Lord has told me that He created you with one purpose in mind—that you would be the woman to reach all of China for Jesus. First, He is going to use you to reach the people of Taiwan with the message of the gospel. He will reach them from the top to the bottom—all the way from the leaders in the palaces down to the most humble barefoot peasant working in the rice paddies. And when revival has begun in Taiwan, the door of Red China will be open to you. You will go in to minister to your Chinese people—one-fourth of the world's population. You will win them for Jesus. He will use Taiwan as the door to break through to the whole country of Red China. Thus saith the Lord."

I was stunned. The man was crazy, out of his mind. I was no Billy Graham. Red China would never be open to me! I shuddered, remembering the ugly face of the Communist at the Shanghai police station who had thrown my exit permit on the floor thirteen years ago and shouted at me to get out of Red China and stay out forever.

But even as I remembered that, I knew that Taiwan and Mainland China would *have* to be won for the Lord by Chinese people. I was aware that many men like Hudson Taylor, Jonathan Goforth, and Robert Morrison had introduced the gospel to China, and that American medical missionaries had given their lives to spread the Word in foreign lands—but I knew it would take Chinese people to really reach the masses in China with the gospel. Americans and others from the Western world are totally different people, from totally different cultures. Their speech is different, their eating is different, their whole way of thinking is vastly different. Even when Americans study the culture of China, even when they learn to use chopsticks and speak Chinese fluently, they still don't "speak the same language" as a Chinese person. They have a completely different way of looking at things. Americans are so honest, they'll tell you what they think. But Chinese are very reserved. They will bow and smile, pretending everything is all right, when it really is not.

As I thought about these things, all my inner arguments against God using me in Taiwan started to shrivel up and die. I knew He *could* use me there, but He would have to open the doors. He would have to plan the whole thing.

"You go," He seemed to agree, "and I will go with you. I will make the way."

As for going to Red China someday, that was too preposterous even to consider.

Outwardly then, I began to make halfhearted plans to go to Taiwan. But inwardly, I was still dragging my feet, only half-yielded to His plan. The other half of me wanted to stay at home, to be with my children every day, to see Ruthie and Paul and Joe come home from school in the afternoon, to watch them eat their snacks and study their homework. I wanted to be at home with them in the evening, to tuck them into bed and to hear their prayers. The mother's heart in me had no desire to leave them for some place halfway around the world, and I told them so.

But I had to go, like it or not.

One morning I told Ruth, "I want you to come home from school early today to help me pack my suitcases. You're so good at it, and you know how much I hate to pack. I'm going to Taiwan, but if nobody wants me to preach when I get there, I'll just go to a hotel and eat some good Chinese cooking—I really miss it—and then I'll come home on the next plane."

In my heart, I was really hoping no one would let me preach. And I must have been thinking I could fool God. But He always sees the heart. And He knew I wasn't really ready to go.

Ruth was glad to promise to come home early to help me, and because I was so busy I sent a friend to pick her up from school. About the time I expected to see Ruth walking in the door to help me, the phone rang.

"Mrs. Lam? I'm calling from the emergency room. I'm afraid there's been an accident . . ."

I sank into a chair, and the voice went on to tell me that a car had run through a stop sign and smashed into the automobile in which my daughter was riding. She had been brought to the hospital in an ambulance, was unconscious, and they didn't yet know the full extent of her injuries. The car was a total loss.

"You had better come to the emergency room at once."

Cold fear gripped my heart. All the way to the hospital, I prayed as fervently as I knew how:

"Lord, save my daughter. Lord, save my Ruthie."

When I arrived, the emergency room personnel wouldn't let me in.

"It's best if you wait out here," they said, pointing to a chair in the waiting room. But I couldn't sit down. Ruthie might be dying. For three hours I paced up and down in the cold hallway, waiting, praying, weeping, and repenting before God for the disobedience that had been in my heart.

"Lord, I'm sorry I didn't want to obey You. Forgive me, Lord. Please forgive me."

During the endless waiting, I knew how Jonah must have felt inside the great fish for three days, repenting of his disobedience in not wanting to go where the Lord had called him.

Finally a nurse came out of the emergency room and told me that Ruth had regained consciousness, that X-rays showed no broken bones, and that I could take her home! I was limp with relief. When Ruth was brought out, there were still bits of glass in her hair, and her sweater was torn, but *she* didn't have a scratch. It had to be a miracle! I was so thankful to God that all I wanted to do was praise Him—and please Him.

There were tears in Ruth's eyes as she looked up at me—and the tears were not for herself.

"Mom, why didn't you want to obey God? Why didn't you want to go and preach the gospel to your people in Taiwan? If you don't do the Lord's work, He won't like it. He can take care of you when you go—and He can take care of us kids here at home. You won't need to worry about anything."

I cried and prayed most of the night, and the next morning I told the children goodbye before I left for the airport.

"Kids, I'm going to Taiwan to do the Lord's will. If nobody wants me to preach in the church, I will preach like the Salvation Army—on the sidewalks. If nobody listens, I will still preach, because God has told me to do it. Whatever happens from now on, for the rest of my life, I will obey the Lord. Whatever He tells me to do from this day on, I will always do it."

Many weary hours later, I landed in Taipei, the big, busy, bicycle-and-motorbike-filled capital city of Taiwan. I wondered where the Lord would open a door for me to preach. But preaching wasn't the first thing the Lord had planned for me there.

The front-page news in Kaohsiung was that famous, high-ranking General Wu Sung Ching had been critically injured in an automobile accident. He had been in the back seat of his car when another car had come crashing headlong into it. The General's chauffeur had been thrown through the windshield, and General Wu had suffered broken bones, severe lacerations, and bruises all over his body.

I was a stranger to Taiwan but one of my mother's friends had found out I was there. She knew I believed in divine healing, because my mother had translated Kathryn Kuhlman's *I Believe in Miracles* into Chinese, and they had talked together about such things. My mother's friend told the General's friends about me.

"General Wu's going to die anyway," they said hopelessly, "so there can't be any harm in telling Nora Lam about his condition. Why don't you call her up and ask her if she will come to Kaohsiung to pray for him?"

When my mother's friend telephoned me, I said I would love to pray for him. Hadn't I just seen the Lord deliver Ruth from injury in her accident?

But when I got to the hospital and saw the General, I almost wished I hadn't come. Stretched out on a too-white bed, he was almost paler than the sheets. Looking more dead than alive, he was covered from head to toe with bandages. And the uniformed guards walking up and down with guns at their hips made me feel even more uncomfortable.

I thought of backing out.

If I pay, and God doesn't raise him up, I could be in bad trouble. I might have to get out of this country in a hurry.

That's how I felt in the natural, but in the supernatural, I knew I didn't have to worry about anything. My God was able. He had just proved Himself to me that very week. And I knew His Word promised that the same resurrection power that raised Jesus from the dead was dwelling in me, that I had all the power in heaven and earth to fight the enemy—death.

Reminding myself that I was a servant of the most high God, a daughter of the King of kings and the Lord of lords, I felt my inner man rise up. Whenever that happens, I know the enemy has to flee. So I spoke to all the worried-looking security people pacing back and forth with their weapons:

"I want all of you to leave this room so I can pray," I said.

It took them by surprise.

"Who do you think you are, asking us to leave? We're not going to leave. Why do you want us to leave in the first place?"

"You have a heart of unbelief," I told them. "I cannot

let you remain in this room and hinder my prayer from going to heaven."

They didn't argue, just stood there like statues. I didn't move either.

"If you don't leave, I won't pray."

By that time, I really wanted to pray and see the resurrection power raise up General Wu so that the whole city would know that my God is real. All the guns of the soldiers had reminded me that I had the whole armor of God, and that the Word of God was the only weapon I needed. It would do the work.

"In the name of Jesus . . ."

Suddenly, the guards left the room one by one and closed the door softly behind them.

I opened my Bible, and after reading a few verses of scripture to the General, I said to him, "The doctors say you've been very seriously injured. But our God is real, and I say you're going to be healed. I'm going to pray for you right now. I know He can raise you up, and I have come to ask Him to do it."

Then I laid my hands on his quiet form, from the top of his head to the soles of his feet, praying, "In the name of Jesus Christ, be healed. Be healed in the name of Jesus. In the name of Jesus . . . rise up and walk."

I didn't see anything happen, but I wasn't discouraged. I had come in faith and spoken the words. That was my part. The rest was up to God.

16

PREACHING THE WORD—
WITH SIGNS FOLLOWING

After I had prayed for General Wu, I was faced with the problem of finding a pastor who would let me in his pulpit. It wasn't easy. I began by telephoning ministers, asking if anyone would like to have me talk in his church.

"To whom do you belong?" everyone wanted to know. "With what ministry are you affiliated—Billy Graham, or Oral Roberts, or what?"

My answer to their first question slammed every door tight shut.

"I belong to Jesus," I told them. "I'm here because He has sent me."

Somehow that wasn't good enough. No one invited me to speak in his church. It looked as if I was going to have to go out and preach on the street corners after all. Then I remembered the Reverend Matthew Lee, a pastor in. Taipei whose church Kathryn Kuhlman had helped to build. Maybe he would let me hold a revival. I went to see him.

His first answer to my request was an emphatic no.

"In China, we don't have women evangelists," he reminded me.

"But you're my last hope," I pleaded. And then I explained, "God really called me to come. When I rebelled, He sent a prophet to tell me to come, and I nearly chased him out of my house. But the prophecy was confirmed in my heart—I couldn't get away from it. And then my daughter was in an accident . . .

"Pastor Lee, I didn't come because I wanted to come. I came in obedience to the Lord. And now that I'm here, the Lord wants me to speak in your church."

"No," he said again. "It's true that Kathryn Kuhlman did help us. But you're not officially associated with her, and we've never heard of Nora Lam. Besides, my deacons wouldn't like it if I invited a woman to preach."

I couldn't help what his deacons would like or wouldn't like. By this time I *knew* his church was the one the Lord had chosen.

"You pray about it," I told him. "If the Lord doesn't want you to open the door, you can close it. But if He wants you to open it—"

Matthew Lee agreed to pray. He prayed for three nights:

"Lord, get this woman off my back. If she comes to my pulpit, I'll be forced to resign."

The more he tried to pray me out, the more the Lord told him he should pray me in:

"If you want to resign, then resign. But I want this woman in your pulpit. Open your church. Open your church. Open . . ."

He finally agreed to do it, and scheduled me for six nights of revival—from Tuesday through Easter Sunday night.

Only fifty people came to the Tuesday night service. Shaking so with nervousness I could hardly stand up, I gave them my testimony, pouring out my life story and some of the miracles the Lord had performed in my life. It was the first time I had opened my heart to a congregation of my own Chinese people, and I could just feel the love of God for them.

"Oh, God is so real to me!" I said, the tears streaming down my face. I could see He was becoming more real to them, too.

The next night, the congregation was just a little larger. Almost as soon as the service began, a man stood up at his seat among the people.

"My name is C. P. Ying," he said, "and I must tell you what has happened to me. When I came to this service last night, I had been blind in one eye for many years. As I listened to Nora Lam speak, I felt the power of God come down and touch me. Today I can see! I've been to the doctor, and he has confirmed that my eye is healed of blindness.

"Praise God—I can see! I can see!"

The people sat there stunned. There had never been a healing in that church before, not even any special prayers for the sick.

Word of the miracle spread like wildfire, and on Thursday night the little church was packed. Six hundred people had come to see the power of God at work! Although we had no official "healing line," people swarmed forward to ask for prayer for their afflictions. And no one was disappointed. Many were healed, many more gave their hearts to the Lord.

During that service, I didn't have to decide what to say as I stood before the people. The Holy Spirit told me every scripture to read, every word to say. The whole service seemed like a concert. God was the Conductor, blending everything into perfect harmony for His people.

I felt my ministry would never be the same again. The moment I thought I had "arrived," however, I saw how far from perfection I was. To my surprise I was still capable of arguing with God—even in the midst of that service. I found it out when He told me to do something I considered ridiculous:

"Close the meeting."

"Close the meeting?!" I couldn't believe my ears. "But Lord, we've just begun! And You're doing such wonderful things for Your people! Why do You want me to close the meeting already? It doesn't make sense!"

When I had finished sputtering long enough to listen, He told me, "You've got to make room for Me to move—really move. I want you to go out and rent the biggest indoor stadium in town for tomorrow night."

"A stadium, Lord?"

"The biggest indoor stadium in town."

The news burst from me to the people:

"God just spoke to me!" I said. "He wants me to close this meeting and rent the biggest indoor stadium in town!"

They looked at me as if they thought I was crazy, and the pastor ran to my side.

"Would you please repeat that?" he said. "I don't understand it. What are you talking about? I have already announced revival here for the whole week, and—"

"I know," I said. "But Jesus just told me to close the service."

He was too dumbfounded to say anything else. So was I.

The next day I got in a taxi and asked the driver to take me to the biggest indoor stadium in town. The minute I saw it, I knew God had made a mistake. It was huge! It would seat eighteen thousand people! Everybody would *know* I was crazy if I scheduled a meeting in a place as big as that. After all, I had no board of deacons, no sponsor, no "advance team" to set things up. Billy Graham would expect to send people overseas a year ahead of time to fill up a meeting that size.

"You're right, Nora," the Lord seemed to say. "No *man* can fill a stadium overnight, but by My Spirit, *I* can do it. If you will obey Me, I will save six thousand souls in the stadium this week. I will heal the sick, give sight to the blind, open deaf ears, and heal the wounded hearts . . .''

I still thought it was impossible.

"You do the possible," He said gently, as He had said to me many times before, "and I'll take care of the impossible. Just banish every negative thought from your mind and watch Me work."

"Yes, Lord."

Standing there on the dew-damp grass in front of the stadium, I swallowed hard, took a deep breath, closed my eyes, and said, "In the name of Jesus, I claim this stadium for Your revival this week."

When I opened my eyes, a man was standing directly in front of me with a questioning look on his face.

"What on earth are you doing here?" he asked.

"I have just claimed this stadium for the Lord Jesus Christ to use tomorrow night and Sunday," I told him.

"Well," he said, "you'd better go home and forget all about it, because I happen to be the manager here, and a month ago I rented the stadium for a national ballgame to be held this week. There's no way you can use it."

I told him that using the stadium wasn't my idea, it was God's, and that I'd rather be home with my kids for Easter, but that God was almighty and he'd better let God use the stadium. He didn't know what to do with such a determined woman, so he excused himself to telephone the owner.

I don't know what he said on the telephone or what was said to him. Maybe he learned that all the ballplayers had stomach aches and couldn't come, or maybe their flight had been cancelled. Anyway, he gave us permission to use the stadium.

"How much money do you have?" he asked me then. I knew it would cost a lot to rent a stadium, and I didn't have a dime, but I was too uptight to tell him that. Instead, I looked straight at him and said, "Don't you know that my Father is so rich that He owns all the cattle on a thousand hills?"

"Do you mean to tell me your father is a rich rancher?" I thought his eyes would pop out of his head.

"Oh," I replied, knowing it was true and that the Lord would provide somehow, "my father is much richer than a thousand ranchers."

"Well, then," he said, "I won't need any deposit. Here—let's just sign a contract."

His reaction to the Word of God gave me the courage I needed to go to the highways and the byways and invite everyone to come. I got on radio and television to announce the meeting, and I told the people that Jesus was raised from the dead on the first Easter and that He is the same yesterday, today, and forever.

Next, I arranged for a huge ad on the front page of the newspaper. It would cost thousands of dollars, I knew, but since everyone thought I was a millionaire, nobody asked for a deposit. I just signed and signed and signed for all the publicity.

Overnight, the Lord packed the stadium, just as He had promised.

Standing before such a huge crowd, I was scared all over again. Nobody knew me, nobody had ever seen me before. I had no one sponsoring me, no one standing beside me or behind me. Except Jesus. And He was all I needed.

When I opened my mouth and began to speak about the Lord, all of a sudden people began to leave the bleachers and rush forward, pushing wheelchairs they didn't need any more. I saw lepers healed, goiters disappear, blind eyes open. Over one hundred healings of cancer were later verified by the hospital in Taipei, and people wrote me letters about what the Lord had done for them in that meeting. Furthermore, I learned that, a week after I had prayed for General Wu in Kaohsiung, he had been released from the hospital, entirely well.

It was a real breakthrough in healing for free China. Jesus had touched His people. And there wasn't only healing, there was revival too. By Easter Sunday night, more than six thousand souls had streamed forward to accept the Lord.

God had done something glorious, above all I could ask or think. And I had learned something important: When the Lord tells you to move, don't wait for another day. Don't be afraid. Don't use your common sense. Don't let the devil persuade you it won't work. It *will* work—if you trust Him.

There was even healing for me. As I was closing the last meeting, and people were streaming forward to have me lay hands on them, the surging crowd inadvertently knocked me off the platform. In my fall, I twisted my ankle, injuring it so painfully I could hardly walk.

I was taken by taxi to the hospital, where X-rays and further examination revealed that some tendons were torn, and that it would be weeks before I would be able to walk without pain. I recognized the injury as an attack of the enemy, and resisted him with everything in me.

"Lord," I cried, "after all these people have come here and You have healed them by Your mighty power, are You going to send me home in a wheelchair? Lord, all Your glory will come to nothing . . ."

Wanting all the prayers I could get, I telephoned S. K. Sung, my good Christian friend in the United States, and told him about the accident.

"Nora, I knew it already," he said. At the exact time when I had been hurt, he had been praying, and he had seen a vision in which hundreds of devils were beating me down. As he had interceded in the name of Jesus for my deliverance, he had seen the demons depart and leave me alone.

I knew then, just as he knew, that my healing was close at hand.

The next morning, a woman came to visit me in my hotel in Taipei. When I asked her to pray, she laid her hands on my ankle and said, "Lord, You sent Nora over here to do Your work. It isn't right for her to have to go home in a wheelchair. In the name of Jesus, I ask You to glorify Your name. Please touch her foot with perfect wholeness. In the name of Jesus. Amen."

As she prayed this simple prayer, I felt the power of God come down from heaven and take away every trace of pain. Immediately I was able to get up and walk freely. He had proved Himself to me once again.

When I came home from the mountaintop, I fell headlong into a deep valley. My hands shook. I couldn't hold chopsticks for a week because I was so nervous. I didn't want to go to Taiwan ever again.

"Lord, next year, please don't call me. My next-door neighbor isn't doing half what I'm doing for You. Just let me stay home next year. Send Jim Gerrard to prophesy on someone else."

But even as I said it, I knew I *would* go—and go—and go—until He was ready to say, "Nora, that's enough." And as the years went by, I thought He would never say it.

17

FOLLOWING HIS LEADING

When I preached in Taiwan in 1971, the Lord permitted me to visit the Bethany Children's Home in Taipei. A man named Johnson Han was the director there at that time, and he and the children became so dear to me that they seemed like my own family.

After I had talked to the children about the Lord, and the ones who were not already Christians had invited Jesus into their hearts, I asked them if there was anything they wanted Jesus to do for them. Of course there was. To my surprise, however, they didn't ask for food or bicycles or toys or clothing. Instead, one somber-faced little boy spoke up for the whole group and said, "It's so hot here in the summertime, we would like to have a swimming pool."

"A swimming pool?" I had no idea they would ever ask for anything like that. But all the children were jumping up and down with happy shouting:

"Yes! A swimming pool! A swimming pool! We want a swimming pool!"

When the hubbub had died down, one little girl who had taken a squealing part in the joyful uproar became serious for a minute, and asked me a solemn question:

"Could Jesus really give us something as big as a swimming pool?"

I had already promised them that He could supply all their needs from His riches in glory . . .

"Of course He can," I assured them, wishing I believed it myself. "If you need a swimming pool, and you really and truly believe Jesus, He will get one for you."

At that time, I was such a beginner myself in trusting the Lord for financial needs that I had some serious doubts about whether or not He could handle such a big assignment. I certainly hoped He could. I didn't want the children to be disappointed.

When I returned to the United States, I began telling congregations across the land about the orphans who needed a swimming pool, but my use of the English language was still so limited that the people probably didn't understand what I was talking about. At any rate, several weeks went by, and I had received only a little over three hundred dollars toward the swimming pool. I was really discouraged.

Finally the Lord spoke to me:

"Neng Yee," He said, using my Chinese name for a change, "you have a diamond ring which is now worth nearly six thousand dollars. I want you to give it to help buy the swimming pool for the Bethany Children's Home."

My heart said yes, but my mind said no.

"Lord, some people have lots of rings. Why don't You be reasonable and ask them to give? I have only one ring—a personal gift from my family."

"I know," the Lord said. "That's why I want you to give it. I had only one Son."

When I sent the ring to Taiwan to be sold to finance the swimming pool, people heard about it. And all at once they began to open their hearts and their pocketbooks to the orphans. They donated architectural services, cement, labor, lumber, iron, and everything else needed to build a beautiful Olympic-sized pool for the children.

At the time, I was criticized by many people.

"You're a crazy woman," some said. "So many children are starving all over the world, and you're wasting money building a swimming pool."

But the criticism didn't matter. The children had asked, and God had provided. I didn't know *why* He wanted those kids to have a swimming pool, but I knew He must have some reason for it. And in it, He was teaching me not to question His purposes, not to put my mind above His mind, but just to trust Him.

If I had known *why* He wanted those orphans to have a swimming pool, I'd have given my life to build it. And so would those who criticized me most. But I wasn't to know His reason for seven long years.

In the meantime, late in 1971, I felt I had to know the Lord's will—unmistakably—for one of the most crucial decisions of my life. And so I began to fast and pray and seek His face. From December 2, 1971, until January 2, 1972, I ate very little food—my weight dropped thirty pounds—and I spent a lot of time in prayer, because the matter to be decided was such an important one:

Should I remain single, or should I remarry?

I knew I'd be criticized by many people if I, a divorced woman in the ministry, remarried. But I wasn't interested in theories, nor in the opinions of men. I wanted God's will for my life. He was the only One to whom I could afford to listen. He was the only One who knew every detail of the circumstances—that both the man and I had more than ample scriptural grounds for our divorces, that we had both gone far more than the second mile, repeatedly, to try to be reconciled with our former spouses, that we had both suffered unbelievable abuse at their hands, that both of us had a strong background in the tradition that says divorced people are not free to remarry . . .

I had met S. K. Sung in 1958 when I escaped to Hong

Kong; he was the cofounder of a church there. I had seen that he was a really sincere man of God who served the Lord with all his heart, visiting the poor, sponsoring missionaries and evangelists, using his wealth for the glory of God. I had met him again when he immigrated to the United States after I did, and he had encouraged my ministry among the Chinese by paying all the expenses of my 1971 meetings in Taiwan.

But marriage was the furthest thing from my mind—and his—until the Lord began to speak to me about it. And the longer I fasted and prayed and listened for the Lord, the more certain I became that God wanted me to marry S. K. Sung. Near the end of my fast, the Lord sent the old man from my lonely Shanghai childhood to tell me it was His will. And so, in January 1972, Nora Lam became Nora Lam Sung, to the glory of God.

After I had finished my long fast and married S. K., I felt the Lord calling me back to Taiwan already, but I refused to go without real confirmation.

"Please don't send a man to prophesy over me this time," I told Him. "If I'm supposed to go, I want You to confirm it Yourself."

Immediately the Lord began to give me supernatural confirmations all over the country.

The first came one evening when I was talking with a Christian brother. Suddenly the Spirit of the Lord fell upon him and he broke out speaking a language from heaven. Then, as he spoke, the words became more and more clear to me.

"My brother," I asked him, "do you know that you are speaking in perfect Chinese?"

He looked amazed.

"The Lord told me He had something special for you," he said. "This must be it."

The first word among the sounds that were so strange to him was my Chinese name, Sung Neng Yee. The rest of the message was telling me the names of towns in Taiwan where the Lord wanted me to go—Tainan, Kaohsiung, Hualein, Taitung. God said I was to hold crusades in those cities, four nights in each one.

"Lord, I cannot go right now. Wait until after my kids get out of summer school."

"How long must I be patient with you, My child?" He seemed to ask me. "After all the miracles I have done in your life, with how many callings must I call you?"

"But Lord, I just know this is not the right hour. I'm planning . . ."

The Lord let me know, gently, that He didn't need my plans.

Next, he sent me to Las Vegas, where Bernard Johnson, a great missionary to Brazil, was telling the amazing story of two hundred people who had seen the Lord walking among them. All at once, he interrupted his story to say that the Lord had a message for someone in the congregation:

"Anything you want to do for the Lord, you have to do now," he said, and then he went back to telling his story.

I was still resisting with everything in me.

"Lord, Your servant isn't talking to me," I tried to persuade Him. "He's talking about people going to Brazil, and I'm not going in that direction at all."

Again the speaker interrupted himself to minister in the Spirit with a heavy anointing:

"There is a young woman in the congregation. The Lord is speaking to her. She has received the call. This is the hour. If she refuses to go, she will miss the will of God."

Inside, I heard the Lord saying, "This message is for you, My daughter."

I went to the motel and cried and cried. I couldn't eat, I couldn't sleep, and my tears couldn't stop.

"But Lord, I don't want to go yet. I want to wait for later."

"It's not what you want. It's what I want. I want you to go. Why don't you obey Me?"

A few days later, I was visiting an Assembly of God church in San Jose, California. The pastor was preaching about how we could know the will of God for our lives. When he had finished his sermon, he asked everyone who had ever made a commitment to the Lord to come forward.

"And I want Nora Lam to lead the way," he said.

My heart pounded when he called my name, and I went forward with many others and fell on my knees at the altar. As I was pouring out my needs to the Lord, suddenly He told me to stop praying and listen. Immediately I became aware of a woman kneeling beside me, praying in perfect Mandarin, my native dialect. It startled me, because I hadn't noticed any Chinese people in the congregation. Opening my eyes, I saw that the pray-er was Sue Westbrook, an American woman I'd met several years before. I knew she couldn't speak Chinese—but she was doing it! I could understand every word, and the words overwhelmed me:

"Sung Neng Yee, I am coming soon. If you want to do something for Me, you've got to do it right now. I am calling you to Kaohsiung, Tainan, Hualein, and Taitung . . ."

When the prayer was finished, Sue and I fell into one another's arms, and hugged and cried for a long time. Then the pastor brought out a map of Taiwan, and we put pins in the places that had been named in the prayer.

The next day, in another part of California, an American man stood up in the congregation, speaking in Chinese:

"Neng Yee, are you ready to go? The Lord has called you to go to Taiwan."

And then I was in Turlock, California. As I walked into the pulpit, a man standing in the back of the auditorium called me by my Chinese name and said, "My daughter, my daughter, how many confirmations do you need?"

It was more than enough. I fell on my face before the Lord and cried out, "I don't need any more confirmations, Lord. I know it's Your will. I will go."

During the next week I received three more confirmations by letter from overseas:

The first came from a young sister in the Lord in Taiwan. This girl had been my interpreter in 1971. I had never expected to see or hear from her again, but she wrote me saying, "I know the United States is having a Jesus movement, and charismatic things are happening over there. I believe the Lord wants charismatic things to be going on over here too. My church is praying that the Lord will let you come."

The second confirmation came in the form of an invitation to be the principal speaker at a big meeting of WCACA—the World Christian Anti-Communist Association. Seventeen countries would be represented at the meeting. I recognized that the invitation was a miracle because, first, I wasn't famous; second, I was a woman; and third, I was a Pentecostal, and the leaders of WCACA didn't understand anything about the Holy Spirit at that time.

The third letter was from General Wu, who had come to Las Vegas to find me two months after his miraculous healing.

"I was never taught anything about divine healing," he had said then. "But I praise God He had taught you about His power to make broken bodies well again. I want to testify to the whole island of Taiwan that the living God is a God of miracles."

General Wu felt the Lord wanted me to come back to his island.

I knew I had to go. We scheduled the Crusades for October.

18

HIS PROVISION

Now I had a real problem: Where would I get the money? My godly husband, S. K., had paid for the three days of meetings in the stadium in Taipei in 1971, but I couldn't expect one man to underwrite the whole expense of the 1972 ministry.

"Lord, four cities—sixteen days? This thing is so big. I don't know where to raise the money. I don't know the first thing to do."

The Lord reminded me of a number of things:

"When you escaped from Red China, you were a beggar. You didn't have a dime. But your mother-in-law accepted you into her home and gave you four bars of gold."

That was true.

"When the American missionaries needed funds to go on with their revival, I spoke to your heart, and when you were obedient to give them the gold, which was all you had, did you ever go hungry?"

"No, Lord, You provided all I needed. But this is another thing."

"Nothing is another thing, My child. Your faith has to grow. I'm asking more of you now because I have entrusted you with more."

He showed me where I could borrow a thousand

dollars from a relative and send it overseas so people could start setting up the Crusades.

"I'm all you need," He said, "and you're all I need. If you go by faith, I'll support you all the way."

When I mailed the thousand dollars, I knew I would soon need to send four or five thousand more—more than thirty-five thousand altogether for renting stadiums, printing literature, paying telephone bills, and all the rest of it. It was too much.

"Lord, I can't do it."

"Where is your faith today, My child? Everywhere you go, you've been talking about how I got you out of Red China, how I sent My angel to comfort you, how I shut the door of your womb so Joseph could be born in a free land. . . . You talk about all the miracles I have done for you in the past, but where is your faith in Me for today?"

I decided I could afford to trust Him a little longer. And by the fourth of September, two checks had come in for five hundred dollars each.

"This must be the Lord," I said, praising Him for His provision.

"If you'll really trust Me, you'll see better things than this," He promised.

A few days later I was in a meeting with the Reverend Bernard Johnson, who was soon to return to Brazil. I asked him to hold me up in prayer and I would pray for him. After we had prayed, the Lord told me to give the thousand dollars to Bernard Johnson. I almost cried.

"But Lord, this money is to do Your work in Taiwan!"

"The work I want you to do, beloved, is to trust Me and obey Me wherever you are, and not to lean to your own understanding."

That night, I couldn't sleep, I couldn't talk, I was absolutely miserable. By morning, I was ready to surrender. I picked up the phone and called Bernard Johnson.

"The Lord told me to give you a thousand dollars."

For a minute I thought he wasn't on the line any more, because he wasn't saying anything. I jiggled the receiver and called, "Hello—hello—hello—"

He couldn't talk, because he had burst into tears. When he was able to speak, he said, "Do you know what, Nora Lam? The Lord had told me to raise forty thousand. This is the last thousand I need before my departure."

In four months, the Lord gave me all I needed to pay the bills for all the Crusades. And all of it came in ways I didn't expect, because the Lord's ways are better than our ways.

One day, for example, I was praying, "Lord, what church do You want me to go to next?" I had had an invitation to speak at a big meeting on the same day I had been invited to a small one. I couldn't be in both places at once. There would be nine thousand people at the big meeting, and I figured if each person gave just one dollar, I would have nine thousand, but the Lord said, "No. Don't lean to your own understanding, Nora. Depend on Me. I want you to go to the little church in Sparks, Nevada."

The Sunday morning I stood in their pulpit and looked out on the congregations; there were only fifty people present.

"Lord, I need thirty-five thousand dollars, and You've brought me to a congregation with only fifty people!"

"Do you praise Me?"

"Of course I praise You, but—"

"Then don't question what I'm doing; just preach My Word, and signs and wonders will follow."

I stopped looking to man and started turning my eyes upon Jesus, leading the people in worship, then telling them the good news of the Kingdom of God.

When the pastor was saying goodbye at the airport, he handed me a check for $1,144.48.

"This is a miracle," he said. "It proves our people believe that giving is a part of worshiping."

I was so thrilled and excited that I couldn't take time to write a letter. I had to pick up a phone to call one of my workers in Taiwan.

"Don't cry any more," I told her. "The Lord said great things would happen, and they've already started. A little church, with only fifty people, sacrificed to give more than a thousand dollars!"

Two hours later, she walked into a planning meeting with many ministers and told them about the sacrificial giving in the little American church.

"Oh, my brothers," she cried, "it is not the time for us to talk about who is going to sit on the platform, what form of worship we will follow, or whose choir will sing. It is time for us to stop criticizing one another. Just think! Fifty Americans have emptied their pockets to help bring the gospel of salvation to our Chinese people!"

Six denominations apologized to one another for their hardness of heart. They decided to cooperate to charter buses for bringing the people to the Crusade. They expected tens of thousands to come, and thousands of them to be saved. They expected healings, too, and said that, if it was necessary, they were ready to take off the roof to let down the sick people so the Lord could touch them.

And they sent their love to their dear American brothers.

When I heard about it, I wept.

"Lord," I cried, "You're so good to me. I didn't have a way, I didn't have the strength, but You have worked a miracle."

Next God sent me to another small church, where He worked a miracle of a different kind.

"A lot of you will say, 'I will give tomorrow,'" I told them, "or 'I will give when I get rich.' But the Lord has said that time is short." I reminded them how readily they would put two dollars on the table as a tip for a waitress, and how quickly they would spend more than two dollars for hairdos or candy bars or chewing gum. Surely they could give that much each month for God's work in Taiwan.

One woman was deeply moved. She put five dollars in an offering envelope. When we prayed for the offering, she put another five dollars in the envelope. That was all she had in her pocketbook. But as she sat there thinking about how hard it would be to sacrifice two dolars a month, the Lord moved in her heart.

"We say He is real," she told herself, "and we know He is real. If by faith we are saved, and by faith we are healed, we should do everything by faith. If I don't have faith, I had better forget about being a Christian in the first place. If I can't believe God for twenty-four dollars— if my faith is that little—how can I ever make it to heaven?

Suddenly she felt something in her hand. It was money—dollar bills. She counted eight dollars. Where had it come from? Looking around, she saw no one close enough to her to have put money in her hand.

Unless it was an angel.

She put the eight dollars in the envelope and continued to worship the Lord. A moment later, there was more money in her hand. She didn't count it this time, just tucked it into the envelope.

"Oh Father," she cried, "forgive me that my faith was so little when I thought about giving twenty-four dollars. When I think about the big Crusades in the big cities, with a thousand people being saved every night, my sacrifice is much too small! Lord, I want to do more!

"Nora Lam!" she said out loud, getting everyone's attention, "you're asking too little. Why is your faith so small? Why do you ask for only twenty-four dollars from each one? If you ask for $240, the Lord will provide it."

Searching my heart as I stood before the people, I cried, "Lord, my faith *is* too small. Enlarge it. Don't let me hinder the work You want to do. I know if we believe the Bible, the fish will carry the money and we can pick it out of their mouths."

I saw then that I need never worry about money for the Lord's work. He is always able to provide more than enough. All we have to do is believe Him for it.

It was a lesson I would have to learn many times.

It was hot summertime when I got on the plane and went across the sea to hold sixteen nights of revival in Taiwan. The first two nights in Kaohsiung nearly killed me. When I went back to the hotel after the services, my dress was wringing wet with perspiration, and I was completely exhausted from preaching and praying for hundreds of people.

Thousands who had already heard about General Wu's healing had walked for miles and waited from four o'clock in the afternoon until ten o'clock in the evening so they could respond to an altar call and receive the resurrected Jesus as their Lord and Savior. Then they went home in peace. The "sign" that had been given when God healed the famous General had brought forth an abundant harvest.

It was the first time in history that 150 different churches had cooperated to sponsor a healing and evangelistic campaign. The mayor attended our services, and General Wu gave his soul-stirring testimony. Record-breaking crowds thronged the stadiums everywhere.

In one city the Chief of Police, a lifelong Buddhist with a reputation for being a strong-willed person, came humbly forward to accept the Lord and pray the sinner's prayer. The forty-year-old daughter of the commander-in-chief of the armed forces in eastern Taiwan was healed of deafness in one ear.

But it wasn't just the high and mighty who were blessed. The lowly had their cups filled to overflowing as well.

One night I was praying for the sick when I saw a young teenage girl coming to the platform carrying her mother on her back. The woman seemed very old, because she was so thin and about to die with leprosy. Her eyes were closed with blindness. She looked so terrible that I was frightened and couldn't make myself touch her. All I could do was back away, holding my breath, trying to hide my horror, and say the words, "In the name of Jesus, be healed. In the name of Jesus, be healed."

The next night a smiling woman walked up on the platform holding the hand of the same teenager.

"I am the woman you dared not touch," she said. "Jesus has healed me."

Her skin was clear. Her eyes were open. She could see. She had a brand-new face.

Everyone knew that God had worked a miracle.

Oh, how I wept before the Lord.

"Lord, forgive me for my unbelief again. Forgive me for my awful pride, my terrible selfishness. And thank You, Lord, for healing her anyway."

Everyone repented when they saw the power of God at work like that. I asked all the ministers to come up to the front and hold hands together so everyone could see we were one in Him.

"Don't fight anymore," I told them. "Love one another, and yield everything to the Lord Jesus Christ, so He can use us all."

Suddenly the Methodists started to love the Catholics, the Catholics started to love the Baptists, the Baptists started to love the Presbyterians, and the charismatics started to hug everybody. All the people of God came together as one in the Lord. They would never be the same.

In one short month in 1972, I saw twenty-two thousand souls added to the Kingdom of God in Taiwan. The mighty hand of God had accomplished what man could never do.

Oh, what a God we have!

19

RADIO!

In 1973, the Lord told me to go on radio and broadcast the gospel to every part of Taiwan and even into the many parts of Red China where people could listen by shortwave radio. And I still hadn't learned that I could never win an argument with Him.

"But Lord, I'm no big radio personality. I don't even know how to operate the machine."

"You don't need to know how to operate anything. Just preach My Word."

"But Lord, I have the worst voice in the whole world. I'm a Pentecostal evangelist, and the people will turn me off the minute they hear me."

"Don't worry about your voice, Nora. Your heart will speak to the people."

"But Lord, it will cost too much . . ."

Oh, how patient the Lord is with me!

"I will provide, My daughter, I will provide. And soldiers and guns and bullets will not be able to stop My Word on a radio broadcast."

How would He provide? He didn't give me time to try to figure it out for myself. I was in my hotel room in Taipei when the telephone rang. The caller was Mr. Lee Shih-feng, Corporation president of the Broadcasting

Company of China. He wanted to see me, so I met him in the coffee shop.

When we shook hands, he told me that his father had been a Methodist minister. Then I learned that Mr. Lee had attended one of the meetings in the stadium in Taipei in 1971 when the power of God had come down and healed hundreds of people. Mr. Lee had been impressed.

"I didn't have anything to do with any of the healings, of course," I said. "You know all of those healings came because of the power of God. But the Lord has told me He wants me to begin radio broadcasting. And if you could sell me time on your stations . . ."

"I'll be glad to let you have time on *ten* stations," he said, "and I can let you have it for only one hundred dollars a day. You'll be able to reach seventeen million people in Taiwan and hundreds of millions more in Mainland China!"

I laughed and asked him to give me a contract before he could change his mind. Later, he was able to increase the number of stations to nineteen without any additional charge. God had provided quickly and abundantly.

My original sound room was a walk-in closet in my home in California, with an old-fashioned reel-to-reel tape recorder someone had donated to the ministry. At first, it seemed like a big undertaking to broadcast once a week to so many millions of people. Sometimes when I sat in the soundproof closet, talking to the tape recorder to do the programs, I wondered if anyone would ever listen to the broadcasts, if any lives would be touched. I didn't wonder long, however. As soon as the broadcasts went out, listeners in Taiwan began to send letters asking for prayer, requesting Bibles, telling how their lives had been changed as they heard the Word of God and invited Jesus into their hearts.

There were even some letters from Mainland China, written and smuggled out at great risk, telling how people hid in attics and basements so they could tune in without so much danger of being overheard by the authorities who were hostile to Christianity.

By 1976, the response to the weekly broadcasts was so great that I began broadcasting every day. And we graduated from the walk-in closet to a much more sophisticated system in which messages were taped and sent by air freight to Taiwan, where they were rebroadcast over the powerful transmitters of the BCC.

One day I received a very special letter marked "PERSONAL—TO THE ATTENTION OF SUNG NENG YEE."

How excited I was to see that the letter was from my old girlfriend, Mei-an, who had grown up with me in Shanghai.

On the night before I left Red China in 1958, she had cried, "Where will you go, Neng Yee? You were born and brought up in China—how can you *live* somewhere else?"

I had held her hand to comfort her.

"I don't know where I'll go," I told her. "But don't worry about me. My father and mother fed those American Christians in the concentration camps, and took them clothes to wear, and washed their feet and loved them. Before my father died, he told me that if ever I needed help, I could go to America and find the green-eyed, blue-eyed people who would love me because they were my brothers and sisters in the Lord.

"I think someday I might find them," I had told her, but I hadn't really believed it.

All those memories flooded my mind as I wept over her first letter—then a second one, a third, a fourth, a fifth, and finally the last one.

"I was so happy to hear your voice the first time on the radio," she wrote, "to learn that my Neng Yee never betrayed Jesus, but that she is still living for Him, and to hear that you found the blue-eyed, green-eyed people to love you.

"I've been tortured many times for my faith," she went on. "There are scars all over my face and body where the Communists have burned me with hot irons. But I still love Jesus.

"And I know it's hard for you, Neng Yee, traveling so much, speaking everywhere, leaving your family at home and giving away thousands of Bibles and praying for hundreds of people. But don't ever be discouraged, my beloved. Never give up the work to which God has called you. Many underground churches have risen up because of your radio ministry. And your broadcast have nourished the newborn Christians and helped them grow. The radio church is the only church a Chinese Christian can have, because it isn't safe for us to gather together to worship God. . . This may be my last letter," she wrote at the end, "but don't cry for me. I've given a Christian friend your address and told her where she can reach you if anything happens to me. I believe they will be coming to get me very soon. And after that, who knows?

"Oh Neng Yee, my last prayer will be that, whatever happens to me, God will bless the church in America and keep the American Christians free, so they can have Bibles and worship God and keep on helping you tell the Chinese about Jesus.

"Let all the Americans know how much we love them, and assure them that we'll meet in heaven some day. May Communism never touch them and take away their priceless freedom.

"Neng Yee, someone is knocking on the door. This *is* goodbye. God bless you forever. My hour has come . . ."

The envelope in which the last letter came to me was addressed in someone else's handwriting, blurred by tears. My own tears splashed on the pages as I sobbed uncontrollably. My body was wracked with pain for her, knowing that sometimes Christians in Vietnam, Cambodia, and China had been tied together, thrown to the ground, plastic bags pulled over their heads to suffocate them, then their heads chopped off before the big bulldozers crushed the still-warm bodies and covered them with earth . . .

As I gave way to the grief that wrenched the heart out of me, my whole body shuddered with the awfulness of Communist oppression. But the awful picture faded as I heard a Voice, loud and beautiful, that drowned out all atrocities everywhere forever:

"Fear not. I am with You always. And I have overcome the world. You will be with Me in paradise."

I knew that Mei-an had heard the Voice too.

20

OBEDIENCE

In 1974, the Lord told me to take a lot of Americans overseas with me. I didn't think that was a good idea at all, so I fought the Lord all the way.

"Why do You want me to take Americans overseas with me? I don't want to be a tour guide, and I don't want to invite them, because they will just be asking for hamburgers all the time."

But the Lord insisted, so I invited them anyway, against my better judgment. American pastors went with me, and their wives, along with deacons, doctors, lawyers, women in Aglow Fellowships, men in the Full Gospel Business Men's Fellowship, even young people—black and white Christians from all different denominations.

To my surprise and great joy, all of them loved the Chinese food. None of them asked for hamburgers. All of them asked for souls.

And when I gave the first altar call of the Crusade, I saw why God wanted the Americans who loved Jesus to be there with me—it was because I *needed* them to help with the ministry! Thousands of Chinese stormed the altar to receive the Lord, to have prayers for healing, to get a Bible to take home with them. One woman could never minister to so many people, but every American Christian was an extension of Jesus.

As they laid hands on the sick, children with polio started to get up and walk, the blind started to see, and crippled people got out of their wheelchairs and ran down the aisle praising God.

Once more, the Lord had proved that His way was right. In the future, I wouldn't think of holding another Crusade without taking along as many Americans as the planes could hold.

Just a few months later, I knew I was standing at the crossroads of my ministry. I saw the needs, but I didn't know how to meet them. Every year, it seemed that the more I did the work of God, the less I knew about how to do it. I didn't want man's advice; I was desperate to hear from the Lord. I wanted to know exactly how He wanted me to conduct His ministry. I wanted to seek His face.

About that time, someone gave me a book called *God's Chosen Fast*. As I read it, I saw I was supposed to fast and pray, and God would show me what to do, just as He had done when I had fasted to know whether or not I should marry S. K.

Because I had starved in China for so long, fasting wasn't hard for me. And after twenty-one days, when the fast was over, God spoke to me:

"Call Pat Robertson."

I knew who Pat Robertson was, because I had seen him on television, and I had read his book, *Shout It from the Housetops*. But I had never met him, and I was sure he had never heard of me.

"Lord," I said, "Pat Robertson's a big shot. I don't want to waste my telephone money calling him. He would never talk to me."

But the Lord didn't change His mind, so I got on the phone.

"Is this Pat Robertson?" When he said yes, I said, "I don't know why, but the Lord told me to call you."

"Is this Nora Lam?"

"How did you know my name was Nora Lam?"

"I was shaving this morning and Jesus spoke to me and told me you were going to call. You don't have to introduce yourself. I stayed up late last night and read your book."

What he said next floored me:

"I need three and a quarter million dollars."

I couldn't even *think* about that much money, let alone help him to get it.

"Let's pray," I said, as quickly as I could, thinking that praying wouldn't cost me a dime. And, while we were praying, I saw money coming down from heaven like a snowstorm.

"Is it snowing in Virginia?" I asked Pat.

"No."

I told him what I had seen, and that God was telling me it meant that he would soon have all the money he needed. Pat began to praise the Lord, and he kept on praying in tongues and praising the Lord for half an hour or so—on my phone bill, from clear across the country. When he finally said Amen and Goodbye and we hung up, the Lord spoke to me:

"The Lord has a special calling on you, Nora. You have heard the need. Do you have a thousand dollars in the bank?"

I couldn't lie to God. Since He could see inside safe-deposit boxes, He probably knew my bank balance too.

"Yes, Lord, I have a thousand dollars, but it's not for Pat Robertson, it's for China. Besides, my little thousand would never help Pat—he needs three and a quarter million."

"Don't worry about how much he needs, just do your part, and I'll do Mine. I'm the One who owns the money in your bank account, and I want you to be My book-keeper and transfer that money to Pat Robertson."

I was sick about it, and wished I'd never heard of him, but I picked up my pen and wrote him a letter.

"Dear Pat Robertson, I will probably never call you

again as long as I live, but I'm sending you a thousand dollars." Oh, how I hated to do that!

At the same time God was speaking to me, He was speaking to Pat, too.

"You have a great need, don't you," the Lord said to Pat, according to what he told me later. "If you want your need to be met, send ten thousand dollars to Nora Lam Ministries."

Pat hadn't expected my phone call to cost him ten thousand dollars but he agreed to give me the money. Then he told me to jump on a plane and fly to Virginia Beach to be on the "700 Club" TV program. On the program, I told everybody about my thousand and Pat's ten thousand that had changed places with each another. And I made a confession.

"I used to think that Oral Roberts was hungry for money," I admitted. "I thought he preached about seed faith all the time because he wanted people to send him their dollars. But now I have seen for myself how it works. He knew God would help the people who planted seeds. I would have planted a seed long ago if I had known it would grow so quickly."

After I told the story, people started sending lots of seeds to the Christian Broadcasting Network. When I got home, Pat wrote me a letter and sent me *another* ten thousand, because God had already supplied the three and a quarter million—*plus* an additional $178,000!

All of a sudden, I had twenty thousand dollars I didn't already owe to somebody. I knew God had a big plan for it.

"Lord, what do You want me to do with this twenty thousand?"

"I want you to charter buses and bring twenty thousand school children from idol-worshiping Buddhist families to your next Crusade every afternoon. They have never heard the name of Jesus, and I want you to tell them about Him."

We chartered the buses, and the children came. They were *hungry* to accept the Lord, and stretched out their little hands for the Bibles we gave to each one so they could read more about Jesus.

That week, twenty thousand children went home as missionaries to forty thousand idol-worshiping parents and told them about Jesus.

I was glad I had called Pat Robertson after all.

But when the 1975 Crusade was over, I went home dissatisfied. We had reached many people for the Lord, but a crusade is only once a year. And that wasn't enough. Yes, there were the radio broadcasts every day, and they were accomplishing a lot, but I wanted to do more.

"Lord, please show me how I can do more and better for You."

"Go and buy TV time," He said.

For the first time in my life, I didn't argue. I knew I didn't know a thing about television, but I knew I didn't have to know anything. I just had to do what God told me, and He would take care of the details.

I made a reservation right away and flew to Taiwan and went straight to the office of China TV. The man in charge of selling TV time could hardly believe I had done such a thing.

"Why didn't you call me long distance instead of making such a long trip?" he asked me. "And how did you know I would sell time to you? The gospel has never been on China TV before. There are not that many Christians here—only three percent of the people."

"I know," I told him. "I came in person instead of calling, because the Lord told me to come. I guess He knew that if I called you long distance you'd say no. You'd tell me that you couldn't sell TV time for a gospel program."

He shook his head. I could tell he was disgusted with me.

"I can't give you a contract to buy time," he explained. "I can't sell it to you."

"Yes, you can," I insisted, "because God told me to buy it."

"You come on too strong," he said. "It makes people not like you."

"Well, I'm sorry if they don't like me. But when God tells me to do something, I have to do it, whether anyone likes me or not. I have to do my Father's business."

I was determined to sit there until he had given me what I had come to get. I could see he wanted to change the subject, to get me off the track.

"Somebody who came to your Crusade this year is really mad at you," he said.

"Who's mad at me?" I didn't think I had done anything to make anyone angry.

"There was a man who had a malignant brain tumor," he said. "He came to your crusade, but he had to wait three whole days before he had his chance to get on the platform for you to pray for him. Since he had waited so long, he thought you would spend a few minutes, at least, praying for him. But all you did was touch him on the head and say, one time, 'In the name of Jesus, be healed.'

"He was so disappointed that he went home and got angrier and angrier that he had wasted so much time waiting for a real prayer, and you only prayed one short sentence. Finally, he went to bed, and during the night he started perspiring all over. The inside of his head got so hot that when he looked in the mirror he almost thought he saw smoke coming out of his ears. He didn't know what was going on.

"The next morning, he went to the doctor to find out what was happening. The doctor gave him an examination, made some new X-rays, and told him the tumor had disappeared without a trace."

That sounded like good news to me, not something to be mad about, but I kept quiet, wanting the man to discover it for himself.

He still sounded disgusted when he told the end of the story:

"Now the man says he wants to get on TV and tell the whole world about his healing."

The man in charge of selling TV time sat and looked surprised and thoughtful for a minute. I know he had been using that story to condemn me, but I could see the Holy Spirit turning it around and using it to convict him instead.

"I guess I should not fight you," he said, looking almost mystified.

"I guess not," I agreed.

"I guess I should sell time to you."

"I guess so," I said.

We signed a contract for the first gospel program on TV in the history of Taiwan!

I was so excited that when I got back to the lobby of my hotel I had to spread the word around:

"We're going to get on TV with the gospel in Chinese for the first time in the history of the world!" I shouted for everyone to hear.

People dropped what they were doing in the coffee shop and in the bar and came running to see what all the commotion was about. In the midst of all the joyful confusion, a young woman in her twenties shoved everyone aside and came up to me, putting her hand on my arm.

"Are you the voice who broadcasts to Taiwan on the radio every day from the United States?" she asked.

"Yes," I told her, "but how did you know?"

"Two years ago, I was blind," she said. "I was on the verge of killing myself, when I suddenly heard your voice on the radio talking about somebody called Jesus who could make the blind to see. Right then, I knelt down and asked Jesus to come into my life, and He healed my blind eyes too."

Oh, it was so beautiful to know that God was using the radio broadcasts in such a wonderful way, that I wasn't just talking to myself when I taped the messages. And I didn't have long to wait to learn that He could use the television in a mighty way too. When the man who had had the brain tumor gave his testimony on one of our first half-hour programs in 1976, we received two thousand letters from the mountains, the valleys, the little villages, and even all the way from the farthest frontier in Taiwan—people were writing to say they had seen the program, they had accepted the Lord, and they had been healed by the power of the mighty God.

I stuffed the avalanche of mail into a suitcase to take home with me. When I was going through customs at the airport, the official in charge demanded, "What are all those letters?"

"Those aren't letters," I told him. "They are the souls of China."

When a Crusade gets underway, crowds throng into huge stadiums. In 1977, umbrellas were everywhere *(above)*.

Then came the typhoon. The destruction was unbelievable. The place where the American team had been sitting the night before was demolished, and our Bibles were waterlogged. I wept *(left)*. Then we made plans to clean up the debris and go on with the Crusade *(below)*.

Top left: The 1978 Crusade in Taipei was held in a huge soccer stadium.
Bottom left: When the invitation was given, people who wanted to receive Jesus came running. Chinese of all ages and sizes flocked to the front to receive the Lord. *Above:* No one was too young—or too old— to be born again.

Right: American Crusade members helped with the ministry. You don't need to know the language if you have the love. *Below:* There were prayers for healing—that the blind might receive their sight, the deaf their hearing, the crippled might walk, the weak be made strong, the diseased be made whole in the name of Jesus. Believers stretched forth their hands in agreement, that the power of God might be manifested—and it was!

It was a real joy for me to share Christmas day, 1978, with the children of Bethany Children's home. Ruth and I brought gifts for the children *(right)* and I told them the wonderful story of Jesus' birth *(below)*.

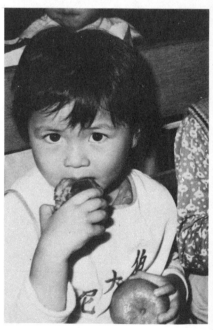

When the American team members went with me to visit the Mountain Children's Home, the children lined up to greet us. Later, dressed in their colorful costumes, they did a tribal dance to entertain the visitors.

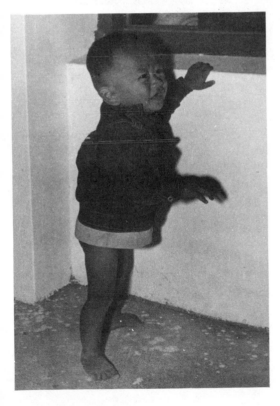

My heart goes out to children everywhere.

Left: At the refugee camp on Makung Island, my daughter comforted one of the precious children, while an old woman told me about her perilous trip, and how she survived.

We distributed Bibles and prayed with the refugees. *Above:* Two of the boat people began to read their new Bibles with great interests. A Chinese begins to read at the back of the book, of course.

Communist Chinese squadron commander Colonel Fan Yuen-yen defected to Taiwan in his MIG-19 fighter jet to join the Nationalist Air Force. When I interviewed him in 1978 on my TV program and learned about the conditions existing behind the Bamboo Curtain, my heart wept for my people.

Distributing Bibles is an important part of Nora Lam Ministries. *Above:* The Living Bible in Chinese. *Below:* On Quemoy Island in 1978, I helped soldiers pack Chinese Bibles into waterproof bags; balloons would carry them deep into Mainland China. Even after normalization Christian tourists carrying Bibles could never go to all the places the balloons go.

Above: When I visited Red China in 1979, I met with some Christians from the underground church. In a hotel room, my companions and I had our picture taken with some of these Chinese believers.

Standing out in my memory from the China trip were this Communist soldier and this toothless old woman with her broken wheelbarrow of vegetables. Both of them need Jesus. I want to go back and tell them about Him.

21

GLORY

What was the year? I really don't remember, and it doesn't matter, because what happened is forever.

I had just arrived at the Taipei airport, and reporters were there to meet me. They wanted to hear all the details of my visit to Taiwan, so I decided to hold a press conference on the spot.

I was answering questions while the flashbulbs popped, when I heard a disturbance at the edge of the crowd. I could see a thin, frail woman trying politely to push her way to the front. A whole cluster of stair-step children were following close behind her, while the people tried to hold them back.

What was it all about?

"I must see Nora," the woman said, trying to be heard above the noisy crowd. "I have brought her a gift, and I must talk to her."

I held up my hand and asked the people to let her through. I counted nine stair-step children sticking close to her sides. Shyly she approached me and thrust a bedraggled bouquet of wilted flowers into my hand.

"I heard you would be here, and I wanted to meet you," she said softly. "I wanted to come to thank you for what you have done for me and my family."

I had never seen her before, so naturally I wondered what she was talking about. She looked full of joy, but so tired that I found a place for her to sit down. While everyone listened, she began with an apology:

"I'm sorry the flowers have died. They were beautiful when we picked them for you before we left home four days ago. And I'm sorry that the children and I are so dirty from our journey."

As I looked down on them and smiled, some of the little ones grinned bashfully, giggled, and tried to hide behind one another.

"It was just about a year ago . . ."

With that, Lee Sung Yu held me spellbound as she told a tragic story of a life that had become so unbearably difficult for her that she could see only one way out. Giving up all hope, she had made a final, horrible decision. She would cook a last meal for her precious children and, beginning with the oldest, take them one by one to a deep well near the wretched hovel they called home and throw them in the well to die. Then she would jump in herself, and be through with hunger and sorrow and pain forever.

Trembling with the horror of her plan, she told all of the children to come with her to the well. As they obediently followed her, never suspecting what was in her mind, one of the boys couldn't resist picking up their tiny transistor radio and sticking it inside his ragged shirt. Turning the dial, he accidentally tuned in to one of my radio broadcasts. As they all walked together toward the well, Lee Sung Yu heard my voice speaking directly to her:

"I'm the mother of three children. I was persecuted and tortured by the Communists, but God performed a miracle to let me escape from Red China. Mothers, wherever you are, let me tell you that Jesus, the Son of God, is the answer to all your problems. No matter how discouraged you might be right now, He can give you hope. Don't give up; just wait on the Lord. He will help you. You and your kids belong to Him. He wants to take care of you."

As Lee Sung Yu listened, the Holy Spirit did a work in her heart. Sobbing, she fell to her knees beside the well and cried out to God:

"I'm so helpless, so alone! Do for me what You did for the lady on the radio. You can have my life—but help me, and help my children!"

She rose from her knees a new creature in Christ, knowing that with Jesus in her heart she could face the future, whatever it held.

On the day when she had planned to end the lives of her children, she introduced them instead to the One who gives everlasting life.

That was all very wonderful, but it wasn't the end of her story. As she continued to listen to her radio in the days that followed, she learned more about how to share her faith in Jesus with others. She memorized some of the scriptures I read over the air. Then she began to travel on her dilapidated, rusty bicycle up and down the little streets of her village, sharing Jesus with everyone who would listen.

That was what she had come to tell me—how one tiny Chinese mother, so near suicide one day, had in a single year led most of her village to Jesus.

Burying my face in the bouquet of wilted flowers—the most precious bouquet I had ever seen—I wept for joy.

"Oh God! Don't let me ever give up! I want to tell the good news of Jesus everywhere forever, even if it costs me my life."

22

TIME OF TROUBLES—AND JOY

Early in 1977, God gave me a vision for the next Crusade. He said to me, "Reach the leaders; reach the children; use the media."

Obedient to the vision, S. K. and I went to Kaohsiung in late March to make arrangements for the big meetings that would be held there later in the summer. We invited the mayor of the city and other important leaders to sit on the platform; we rented seven hundred buses so that we could bring the children in from all over the city as well as from remote mountain areas; and we arranged for the Christian Broadcasting Network to videotape the whole Crusade for later presentation on our television program.

Once again, we knew that if we would be faithful to do our little part, God would do His big part.

That was especially important for me to remember on April 1, when the overseas telephone rang in our hotel room with terrible news. My mother had been rushed to the hospital. She was in critical condition, not expected to live.

I was eight thousand miles away—I couldn't possibly get home in time to tell her goodbye. I fell on my knees to ask God for a miracle:

"Lord, you know how much I love my mother. You know how close we have been ever since she adopted me when I was a tiny baby. Lord, You know I couldn't bear it if I went home and she was gone already. And Lord, she's been praying so faithfully for her son Neng Yao to get out of Red China. Surely You wouldn't take her home without letting her see the answer to her prayers . . ."

I cried before the Lord and asked Him to raise her up. Then God told me to call Pastor Ralph Wilkerson at Melodyland and ask him to go pray for her. He said he would get a private plane to fly him to San Jose immediately.

A few hours later, another phone call brought the news that my mother's heart had actually stopped beating, but when Pastor Wilkerson had laid hands on her and prayed, she had opened her eyes, fully conscious, and thanked him. From that moment on, she had begun to recover and grow stronger.

My mother's miraculous recovery strengthened my faith that Neng Yao would get out of Red China, because I knew the Lord doesn't start something and give up. He finishes what He has begun. Everywhere I went from then on, in Taiwan and back in the United States, in churches all over the country, I asked people to pray for my brother's release.

1977 seemed to be a time of troubles that the Lord would use for His glory. The very day I was to leave the United States for the July Crusade, my mother fell and broke her hip. I rushed her to the hospital, where I had to leave her so I could finish packing and go to the airport. She knew I had no choice, and was very brave about it, even though she was in considerable pain. I was so sad that I cried all the way to Taiwan.

On Sunday afternoon, July 24, the opening day of the Crusade, a steady rain began to fall. The weather reports said Typhoon Thelma was threatening the area, but that didn't stop the people. The first meeting wasn't scheduled to begin until seven thirty in the evening, but people began to arrive at four o'clock in the afternoon, in spite of the rain which wasn't letting up, but getting heavier by the hour.

The 175 Americans who were with me for the Crusade were impressed that the Chinese would flock to a meeting in an outdoor stadium when the weather was so bad.

"We can't believe our eyes," they said. "In America, at the first sprinkle, everyone would have decided to stay at home."

The rain came down, but the crowds continued to come, starved to hear the Word of God. Oh how hungry they were to have an opportunity to receive Jesus as their personal Savior so He could help them walk daily in a life of joy and victory.

Soon the stadium was packed, with over thirty thousand people pressed tightly together in the wet bleachers under their umbrellas. And still the people came—until there were many more standing under the bleachers and outside the stadium where they would be able to hear the message on the loudspeaker system.

When I gave the altar call about nine thirty that night, practically everybody present raised their hands to say they wanted to pray the sinner's prayer and invite this Jesus into their hearts. They literally ran toward the altar until there was no more room to run. And as they accepted the Lord, they stretched out their hands to receive the thousands of Bibles being passed out by their new American brothers and sisters in the Lord.

Later that night, Kaohsiung was hit with all the fury of one of the worst typhoons in its history. There were winds of 125 miles per hour, and a torrential downpour. The force of the wind shook my hotel room, where the windows were lashed with the driving rain. Soon the hotel management made everyone leave their rooms and go to the lobby, and then to the basement, because they were afraid the windows would crash to pieces at any minute.

After the storm subsided, ten members of the Crusade team went with me to the stadium to look at the damage. The destruction was unbelievable; the stadium was a complete wreck. The colorful bandstand where the mayor and other leaders of the country had been seated the night before had been completely demolished. In utter despair, we left the stadium and went to the indoor arena where we had been planning to hold the Children's Crusade in the afternoon. We saw that, even there, part of the roof had blown off, and there was water and windblown debris everywhere.

Some thought we should give up and go home. Under the circumstances, no one could blame them. In the aftermath of the storm, business-as-usual was unthinkable. Our hotels were without electricity or running water. It would be days before service could be restored. There was no way to print a newspaper, no telephone service so we could contact anyone . . .

"God must be planning to do something big," we tried to encourage one another. "Otherwise, why would the enemy be trying so hard to stop us?"

I cried to the Lord, "Oh God, I didn't come here to impress Americans, or Chinese leaders, or the children, or anybody. I came because You sent me, and because the Spirit of the Lord has anointed me to preach the gospel to the poor and to set the captives free from their bondage. Help us, Lord, to be true to You. Don't let a storm make us give up. You're bigger than any storm."

He seemed to say, "Don't be afraid, Nora. As long as you have a broken and a contrite spirit before Me, My work will be done."

Almost at that moment, when most of the team members were shaking their heads in discouragement, not certain what they should do, three busloads of children from the mountains arrived in the parking lot outside the stadium.

"We drove for hours," the teacher riding in the first bus told us. "The winds wanted to blow us off the highway, and sometimes the rain was coming down so hard we could not see out the windows. Many times the driver and I wanted to turn back, as some buses had done already, but the children wouldn't let us do it.

"'We want to go hear about Jesus,' they told us. 'We want to go and hear about Jesus.'"

We knew God would never disappoint children to whom He had given that much faith. Team members and I got on the buses and gave Bibles to all of the children. Some of the Bibles were soggy from the rain that had blown into the stadium, but the children received them as joyfully as if they hadn't been damaged at all. And with tears in our eyes, we promised them that if they would spend the night in Kaohsiung and come back the next afternoon, with God's help there would be a meeting after all.

When the buses left with the children, who were planning to return for a Crusade the next day, we returned to our hotels to get the other members of the Crusade team. When we told everyone about the faith of the little children, they were ready to roll up their sleeves and get to work—clearing away the debris from the arena, sweeping water out of the building, and rigging up a temporary lighting and sound system.

The next afternoon more buses arrived, and thousands of children became official members of the family of the King of kings.

During the rest of the Crusade, our light and sound systems were strictly makeshift, and rain poured through the hole in the roof, but the glory of the Lord was not dimmed. And despite the destruction of many buildings in the city and the impossibility of normal travel, thousands came to hear the Word of God and to receive Jesus as their own.

There was salvation, and there were healings, and miracles happened before our eyes. Tens of thousands of Bibles were put into hands eager to receive them.

On the way home, I thought about the vision God had given me months before the Crusade began:

"Reach the children." He had done that above all we could ask or think. Furthermore, those three busloads of children with faith that wouldn't give up had reached our hearts, too.

"Use the media." Cameras had captured all the highlights of the most dramatic Crusade of all for use on our TV program.

"Reach the leaders." Had that been accomplished? God reminded me that on the last night of the Crusade the mayor of Kaohsiung, who had been a Buddhist all his life, had held a copy of *The Living Bible* in his hand and proclaimed, "This is the Word of God. We must get it to our people."

Yes, by the mighty working of His Spirit, God's vision was being fulfilled. Nothing had been able to stop it.

A few weeks after we returned home, God showed the greatness of His power in another way. There was an urgent phone call from Taiwan. On September 24 another typhoon had struck the island, with drenching rains and winds of terrifying speed. During the night, the Bethany Children's Home had become flooded. The children woke up screaming in terror, as the murky water swirled around them. They climbed from their bottom bunks to their top bunks in an effort to escape, and still the water rose, almost as if it were pursuing them. Huddling together in fear, they decided on the only course of action that could have saved their lives.

The big kids put the little kids on their backs, dived into

the floodwaters, and swam out of the flooded rooms and across the campus to safety in another building on higher ground. Not a single child was lost. All were good swimmers because of the swimming pool.

How I wept when I heard the news—tears of joy that He had saved the children, and tears of shame when I remembered how reluctant I had been to part with a diamond ring so God could accomplish His purpose.

A few weeks after the flood, I had a letter from Johnson Han.

"Seven years ago," he wrote, "people thought you were crazy. But God knew that in seven years the flood would come, and because of the swimming pool which had turned all the children into little fish in the water, He was able to save their lives."

Johnson Han went on to say that, when the children had reached safety and learned that all their possessions had been destroyed in the flood, the first thing they had said was, "Tell Mama Sung"—that was what they called me—"to send us some new Bibles, because we know it was Jesus who built the swimming pool and taught us to swim so He could save our lives."

23

NENG YAO

In mid-January 1978, I had an opportunity to interview on my TV program a military man recently escaped from Red China. Colonel Fan Yuen-yen was a Chinese Communist squadron commander when he defected to Taiwan in his Mig-19 fighter plane in July of 1977, so he could join the Nationalist Air Force of Free China.

His face clouded as he related the terrible conditions from which he had come. The vast majority of the population was living like animals, he said, in the worst possible starvation conditions. Some people were even giving away their children in exchange for food coupons. One of the Colonel's reasons for defecting had been his horror at seeing children and elderly people gathering around the officers' mess hall to fight over leftovers and other food scraps intended for pigs because they were not fit for human consumption. He told me it was not at all uncommon to see dead human bodies floating down the rivers.

"The people are miserable," he said, "living in constant fear. The Communist hierarchy is unstable, and the army is frequently called out to quell disturbances. There is no freedom, no democracy in Mainland China," he continued. "What foreigners have seen on their visits is a carefully controlled view, a painted façade hiding the stark reality of a dark hell."

When I asked him why he had left his wife and four children behind to risk his life to fly for freedom, his words were eloquent:

"There comes a time when everything is sacrificeable if there is a chance to change things. As a squadron commander I could have soon retired and lived comfortably. But I saw what the Communists were doing, and I saw their increasing success in getting support from the free world. I knew that if someone didn't tell the truth, the Communists would not be stopped until all the world was living in wretchedness and misery. I wanted to tell what I knew before it was too late.

"Please believe me. I am risking my life in order to warn the free world of dangers that will someday destroy every country the Communists touch."

How it hurt me to hear those things and to know that my brother and his wife and child were still living in the midst of the Communist oppression. I was so thankful to know that hundreds of Christians all over the United States and Taiwan were faithfully praying for Neng Yao's release, and that God was hearing every prayer.

One day He spoke to me and said, "Nora, listen carefully, because I'm about to tell you something important. Prepare to receive your brother Neng Yao and his family, because I'm moving to set them free."

Oh, what wonderful news!

About that time, a house directly behind our house in San Jose was for sale, and we were able to buy it. Other people who needed a place to stay lived with us from time to time, and there wasn't room for all of them in our house. S. K. and I had adopted four little orphan girls by that time—two of them from Taiwan and two from Korea, all of them under six years old, so our house was nearly bursting at the seams. The extra house would be

useful for housing the overflow of guests until Neng Yao
and his wife needed it for a temporary residence before
they could get settled in a place of their own. The
backyard of the house joined the backyard of our house,
so we would be able to help take care of them like one big
happy family.

After we bought the house, I didn't know anything else
we could do until Neng Yao was actually on his way to
us. How long that seemed to be taking!

Then one day my daughter-in-law, Paul's wife Susie,
telephoned me—so excited she could hardly talk:

"Mom, mom! I just heard on the television news that
Senator Ted Kennedy is going to Mainland China! You
need to call him and ask him to help get your brother
out!"

I thought she was crazy at first. Who was I to pick up a
phone and call a United States Senator? He didn't know
me. His secretary would just tell me the Senator was too
busy to talk.

"Mom," Susie pleaded, "it couldn't hurt to try."

While I was resisting her suggestion, the Lord reminded me of something I should have learned long ago:

"Nora Lam, who are you to think you are nobody? I
live inside you, and you are My child. Don't be afraid to
telephone anybody when that's what I'm telling you to
do. Don't underestimate who you are. I'm no respecter of
persons, and I don't want you to be either.

"You've been praying for Me to help you in this case?
Well, I *am* helping, but you've got to do your part. Unless
you step out in faith, the Spirit cannot act. The Spirit
wants to save and deliver the whole world, but He waits
for the missionaries to go tell the people the good news. A
telethon doesn't work to bring in money to spread the
gospel until someone rents the auditorium, hooks up the
telephones, and tells the people why they need to give
the money. Lots of times My Holy Spirit wants to do

something to help you, but He cannot move until you move."

I was persuaded. I called the Senator's office. His assistant wanted to know what he could do for us. I told him that I wanted to get .ny brother out of Red China and needed the Senator's help. He told me to send all the details by telegram at once, and he would see what could be done. But he warned us not to be too hopeful because, in the Bay area alone, more than twelve thousand families had applied for relatives to get out of Red China. And there were thousands of other applications from all over the United States.

In the natural, it seemed quite hopeless. But thousands had prayed, God had spoken, and we had done our part.

Several weeks passed, and I learned that the Senator had personally contacted Communist China's Minister of Foreign Affairs about our request. Several more weeks passed, and I learned that Neng Yao and his family had been permitted to travel as far as Canton, but they didn't have the exit permits that would let them leave China. This time, I didn't send any telegrams to anybody. I knew God was working it all out.

For many days, there was no further word. January passed, February, March, April . . . still no word. But I knew Jesus was working.

On May 1, God said, "You will receive news from your brother within a month. He is going to be released from Red China."

Naturally, I told everybody.

Some people who heard the news were jealous.

"How come you hear from the Lord so specifically all the time, and He never tells me anything?"

I didn't know the answer, but I told them I believed that many, many times the Spirit of the Lord is talking, but we are so busy talking ourselves that we don't give our ears a chance to hear Him.

On May 13, the day before Mother's Day, I received a letter from Neng Yao. He said that, all of a sudden, the Communist police had called him up and told him that he and his wife and their baby should get ready to leave the country!

There had been months of paperwork, miles of red tape, but he had finally been granted permission to leave—with his family—a privilege granted to very few among many millions of people.

It was like a release from a death sentence.

And *still* some people didn't believe that God could work miracles.

"Even if he is going to get out of Red China," they said, trying to discourage me, "it will be years before he can be approved as an immigrant to the United States. We have a quota, you know."

On June 1, I went to the immigration office to apply for my brother to come to the United States as an immigrant. On June 2, his immigration visa was issued, approved, and in my hands. God had moved another mountain.

Even I could hardly believe that, but it was true anyway.

I wondered how long it would be before the Lord would let us see one another, but I didn't think about it too much. I knew the Lord would finish what He had begun, and I would just have to wait on Him. Meanwhile, there was a lot of work for me to do to get ready for the 1978 Crusade.

24

CROSSING THE RED SEA

The 1978 Crusade was to be the biggest yet. And as usual, I didn't have any idea where the money was going to come from. Early in June, an organization offered to loan me a million dollars. It was tempting to take it, but I knew that borrowed money has to be paid back sometime, with interest. I couldn't afford to borrow a million dollars from anybody.

"Lord, I'm not going to borrow a million dollars. If You want me to have this Crusade, You will have to provide everything I need. Otherwise, I will quit."

Because He had told me to rent a stadium seating fifty thousand people—the same stadium Billy Graham had used for his Crusade two years earlier—I knew I would need at least a quarter of a million dollars, not including the cost of the two hundred thousand Bibles He had told· us to print for giving away.

I was still not a super-spiritual person, just a human being like everybody else. And when I contemplated the size of the task before me, I wanted to chicken out.

"Lord, I don't want to do this anymore. I can't do it."

"Never say you can't. You can do all things through Jesus Christ who strengthens you."

"Lord, I know that, but it's still too hard for me."

"There's nothing too hard for you, because I am with you always. Just trust Me."

"I am trusting You, Lord, but it's still too hard. The buses alone will cost seventy thousand dollars. The stadium is going to be more expensive than ever. And all the advertising and the printing . . . and the Bibles You told me to have printed will cost a fortune, and . . ."

If ever I had felt sorry for myself, I did then.

"Lord, I'm human. And I'm a woman."

"I am Almighty God, and I'll go before you and behind you and I'll keep My hand of blessing on your head. When there is no way, I will make a way."

"All right, Lord."

Since I *had* to hear His voice for every move I made, I started on a long fast again. I fasted and cried before the Lord for forty days, from June 1 until July 10. During the fast, things went from bad to worse. Every time the overseas workers telephoned, they wanted more money. The Lord instructed me to mail them every nickel that came in, not to save back anything for expenses in our San Jose office.

By July 14, I had come to the bottom of everything. The Lord had told me to prepare thousands of letters to be sent to all the people I knew who had supported me in the past, telling them about our financial crisis and asking them to help me. The letters had been printed, the envelopes had all been addressed, but there was no postage.

Furthermore, I didn't have any money in the bank to buy the nine thousand dollars' worth of stamps I needed to mail the letters.

That afternoon God was really about to put me on the line to see if I would believe Him completely or not. My staff was so worried they could hardly breathe. Nobody was talking, nobody was laughing, nobody was singing, nobody was praising the Lord. A little fly buzzing around in my office sounded like a great big jet airplane because the place was so quiet.

I could imagine what they were all thinking:

"What is Nora going to do this time? She had told us to stuff the envelopes and seal them and sort them out by their zip codes, but where are the stamps?"

To try to cheer them up, I reminded them of a story they had already heard me tell many times:

"Remember the orphanage where the kids were all hungry and there was no food?" I said. "And how they all prayed and set the table and sat down and thanked God for the good food He was going to put before them? They couldn't see the food, and they didn't know how God was going to provide it, but they knew they could depend on Him. And as soon as they had said Amen to their prayer thanking Him for it and asking Him to bless it, someone knocked on the door. When they opened it, there stood one of God's people delivering more food than they could possibly eat.

"God had sent the food because they trusted in Him," I said. "The key is not to depend on ourselves or on what we can see with our eyes, but to think about God, how great He is and how wonderful and true His promises are. He will do everything that is necessary. He will send the stamps just like He sent the food," I told them. "Keep working to get the mail ready to go, and God will do His part."

I wanted them to be confident, but I didn't feel confident myself. When I had finished cheering them up, I went into my private office and closed the door. Then I got down on my knees on the red carpet.

"Lord, remember this is all Your business. You told me to write those letters. If You want me to forget about mailing them, and if You want me to cancel the Crusade, it's all right with me. If it's not Your will for me to go to Taiwan, wipe out all the plans. I'd rather stay home with my family anyway."

He seemed to remind me that He never wants us to look backward when we have put our hands to the plow. He wants us to keep going forward. If we're in a battle and go backward, the enemy shoots us. If we go forward, we win.

After the Lord had strengthened me, I went out to talk to my staff again.

"Look," I said, "don't be afraid. Either you trust God is real and will do what He says, or forget it. Either you belong to the devil or you belong to God. If the world says you're crazy, but God says you're okay, you've got a majority.

"When you know who He is and that you belong to Him, nothing else matters. Sometimes we are crushed with problems, and we are afraid we are going to fail. We're even afraid of success, but we don't need to worry about anything. It's all God's business.

"We're all human, flesh and blood. If I told you that I never worried, I'd be telling a lie. I'm just like you. I cry a lot, get worried a lot, get frightened and irritated, just like everybody else. But He always forgives my unbelief—that's what all these things are, really. And the key to getting what the Lord wants us to have is for us to make a way for Him to release His power by forgiving one another and loving one another.

"Anybody in the ministry has hard times and gets all kinds of criticism. Even if you die for your sheep, they will nail you to the cross. Every servant of God goes through all kinds of trials. If you don't love God, nobody will bother you. If you love the Lord, people will make fun of you and say you're just trying to act spiritual.

"In spiritual warfare, beloved, there is no in-between—either you flow with the Spirit, or you faint without the Spirit. We always want to use man's ways to do God's work—but His way is better, and then He gets all the glory. A lot of times we think God is going to be too late because He comes at the last minute, but He's always on time. He's just giving our faith a chance to grow while we trust Him."

I was preaching quite a sermon for their benefit. But God used the rambling words to strengthen my faith too. I needed it.

On Monday morning I went to the post office to get our mail. Sometimes there are many letters in the box, but that day there were only a few. For half a minute, I was ready to die when I saw there were so few letters. But then I remembered that the enemy wanted me to look at circumstances, but God wanted me to keep my eyes on Him.

Mixed in with the usual business-sized envelopes containing bills was a little, wrinkled, funny-looking envelope sealed with tape on the flap. It wasn't one of my return envelopes sent out to our mailing list, and my name was even spelled incorrectly. Shaky handwriting had lettered "NORA LAMB" in blue ink.

I unfolded the piece of crumpled paper inside the envelope and read, "I've never met you and I've never heard you speak. But a week ago the Lord came to my room and told me to send you all my life savings. You can do whatever you want with it. I know it is the Lord."

I looked back inside the envelope to see if I had missed something. There was a little folded-up green piece of paper—a check for nine thousand dollars—exactly what we needed for stamps.

We *really* praised the Lord.

25

FLOODTIDE

"Are you happy now that you have the nine thousand dollars?" the Lord wanted to know.

I was ashamed to admit I wasn't completely satisfied.

"Nine thousand will get me through today, but how about the rest of the expenses for the Crusade? You know it will still cost about a quarter of a million dollars."

He told me that a quarter of a million is just as easy for Him as nine thousand. Nothing is too hard for Jesus. If He could help me on Monday, He could help me on every other day, too.

We were supposed to leave for overseas on the fourteenth of August. By the eighteenth of July, when we still didn't have the money we needed, the devil wanted to discourage me. But I knew my heart was right with the Lord. That afternoon, God spoke to me: "Within three days, I'm going to meet all your needs. There's going to be a breakthrough. I will perform a miracle."

At first it was exciting to wait for the miracle, but by the twentieth I was so tired of waiting that I folded my pillow around my head and cried.

"Lord, I'm too tired to wait any longer," I said. "You can do what You want to do—I'm going to sleep." I crawled into bed and gave up.

At 11:45 the phone rang. A man with a television ministry had just learned that I had been fasting and praying for forty days so God would provide what we needed for the Crusade. Many people thought that was the greatest thing they had ever heard in all their lives.

"If you have planned this whole thing on faith, without a dime," he said, "I want to help you. If you can trust God that much, I want to give you TV time for a telethon to raise the money for the Crusade."

Everything that could be done in the natural for a successful telethon was put into operation. But nothing worked the way it was supposed to work. We started Thursday night, but not many responded. Friday night, nothing much happened. Saturday night, the same thing. Sunday wasn't scheduled, and I almost died.

Just as it looked as if we had failed completely, I felt my inner man rise up. Suddenly I wasn't afraid of anybody, or what they might think of me, or what they might say. I didn't even care whether anyone pledged any money or not, but I wanted to tell them something from the Lord.

I grabbed the microphone.

"I don't mind if you watch me fail," I told the TV audience, "but I'm not going to fail. If you don't give the money I need for the Crusade, God will provide it some other way, because He loves the Chinese people too. He's not willing that one of them should perish, but that all should have a chance to know the Lord."

I told them the story of the Malaysian mountain people who had killed every missionary who tried to go into their area to tell them about God. Everybody was afraid to go to them, because they would shoot them down with arrows before they could open their mouths to deliver the gospel. Then one day one person came down from the mountain and heard that Jesus died for him. He accepted Jesus into his heart, and God gave him a burden for the mothers in the mountain villages who would throw their beautiful fat babies into the river as a sacrifice to the river they thought was God.

He knew he had to tell his people the good news. And he knew it would cost him his life.

One morning at ten o'clock, he put on a red mask and a red coat and red pants, and said goodbye to his Christian friends. He took a Bible and a cross and put them inside the front of his jacket, then got on his horse to ride up the mountain. Just as he had expected, a rain of arrows shot him down before he could get to the top.

But when the mountain leader came to pull the arrows out of his body, he opened the jacket and saw the Bible. Something made him read it. When he told his people that Jesus died for them, they all accepted the Lord. Everyone received eternal life because of one man's sacrifice.

To the people listening on TV I said, "The only reason God has kept America free is that we have shared Jesus with the world. God isn't asking you to make a sacrifice like that. He's only asking that you love Him and reach out to share so He can send that love to thousands of millions of people who don't know the Lord."

Within a few minutes, the telephones were jammed with calls. And within one hour we had pledges for most of the money needed for the Crusade.

God had done it all—His way.

26

GOD'S PROMISE FULFILLED

Overseas preparations for the 1978 Crusade had been going on for months. A committee of two hundred forty pastors, laymen, and government officials gave leadership through nineteen committees to over three thousand volunteer workers. For the first time, plans were made to bring five thousand aborigines from the mountains to the Crusade. One hundred buses were mobilized to transport them from all over the northern half of Taiwan. Two camps—like two small cities,—were set up in schools near the stadium where they could eat, sleep, receive medical help, and have facilities for fellowship and recreation. It would be the first trip into a city for many of them. They were being brought to the Crusade at great expense so they could receive the Lord and go back to evangelize their villages in the high mountainous areas of their beloved country.

Nearly four hundred churches in the Taipei area were participating in the Crusade, many denominations working side by side to reach the lost. Seven hundred buses would bring delegations from the churches to the stadium, crisscrossing the city in a network of routes to provide free transportation for any wishing to attend the Crusade. At invitation time, two hundred trained Chinese counselors and almost three hundred American workers would be on hand to pray with the people who wanted to receive the Lord or have special prayers for physical, mental, or spiritual problems in their lives. Two hundred thousand Chinese *Living Bibles* had been printed, and thousands of smaller, colorful books on the life of Christ were piled, ready for distribution. Five hundred prayer cells had been established all over Taiwan, some containing only two or three persons with the Lord in the midst of them as they prayed. Some had larger numbers, but the same purpose—to be intercessors for those who would come. A month before the Crusade began, the prayer tempo was stepped up, with a twenty-four-hour prayer chain in which hundreds were praying all over the island.

At last it was the opening day of the Crusade in the big Civic Sports Stadium.

In the afternoon, hundreds of buses unloaded swarms of people at the entrances of the massive arena. As darkness settled, huge banks of lights flooded the farthest corners with light. People continued to pour into the grandstands of the great grassy soccer field, with its straight white lines marked on the green.

A large platform had been erected at a central location. Television crews made last-minute adjustments on the cameras which were to videotape the services for future television release. A powerful sound system was set up to convey every utterance to the most distant areas of the stadium in Mandarin and Taiwanese simultaneously.

In the beginning, all rose to sing hymns familiar to the sprinkling of believers in the vast congregation, the Chinese singing Chinese words, the Americans of the Crusade team singing English words to the same music. After that portion of the song service, the colorful aborigine choir sang, then the beautifully robed Mandarin choir. Dr. Ralph Wilkerson of Melodyland Christian Center in

Anaheim, California, presided, and his wife played the organ. Popular singing star B. J. Thomas sang and gave his testimony of deliverance from drug addiction to a new life in Christ. Patti Roberts sang. And finally, I got up to preach the Word of God.

I told them how the true and living God, who had created the whole world, loved them so much that He sent His only Son to die for their sins, so they could live forever. I told them how this real God had been with me in the hard times of my life, and how He had worked miracles to bring me from a place of persecution into a free land where I could worship Him. I told them that God would bless their nation and meet every need in their lives if they would abandon their idol worship and turn to Him. And I told them that Jesus is coming back soon to receive those who belong to Him. They could prepare themselves for that great day by inviting Jesus to live in their hearts.

From every corner of the gigantic stadium, they came running to Jesus, thousands of people of all ages and sizes—mothers with babies tied on their backs, young men on crutches, old men who were sightless being led by loved ones . . .

Lives were changed and renewed, Christians and missionaries were encouraged. Many were healed and restored to health—the lame and the crippled walked, the blind received their sight, tumors melted away, deaf ears heard the Word of God, and the Holy Spirit filled many to overflowing.

Jesus was lifted up, and because that was done, I knew He was powerfully at work to draw all men unto Himself. That great ingathering of Chinese souls into God's Kingdom was like an earthshaking crescendo in God's symphony. It was an experience I will never forget as long as God gives me breath.

Late on August 20, when the Crusade was over for

another year, I went to my hotel room exhausted, and collapsed across the bed, letting my shoes fall to the floor. I was rejoicing in all I had seen the Lord accomplish by the mighty moving of His Spirit.

"Lord, I thank You, *how* I thank You!"

Before I had time to say anything else, the phone was ringing. It was our travel agent for the tour. He said there had been an unexpected rerouting of the flight we would be taking to Manila the next day. Unforeseen circumstances would make it necessary for us to change planes in Hong Kong.

Hong Kong! That's where my brother Neng Yao was going to enter the free world!

I knew the rerouting was no accident, but a provision from God.

Excitedly I called my aunt who lived in Hong Kong, and asked her if there was anything that could be done to speed my brother's arrival into that city. But that was unnecessary—he had gotten out of Red China just the night before and was already in Hong Kong waiting to see me!

When our plane touched down at the Hong Kong airport, I rushed into the terminal building. There stood my brother, his wife, and their little black-haired, bright-eyed son, all three of them grinning from ear to ear.

What a reunion we had! How thrilling it was to shake their hands and stand face to face with Neng Yao after twenty years of praying and wondering whether we would ever meet again. My brother had been just a boy, now he was a man. My heart was about to burst with joy, but we didn't have long together before I had to run to another airline to catch my connecting flight for Manila. I assured him I would be returning soon with tickets for them and all arrangements made to take them to America with me.

By October 1, everything was ready, and I left the

United States for Taipei, where I was to speak to the World Christian Anti-Communist Association again, planning to pick up my brother and his family on the return trip.

There's no room for differences among Christians any more, I told the delegates from ninety nations at the convention. We must love one another, hold our hands together against a common enemy, and share Jesus with all the world while there is yet time. Then I told them about the mighty power of the Holy Spirit, who could accomplish what man could never do.

Heading for home on October 6, I stopped in Hong Kong, joyfully picked up my brother and his family, and flew toward America and freedom.

The first thing I did when I got home from the airport was to take Neng Yao to the room just off the kitchen, where our mother had been bedfast for some time.

"Mama, here is your son," I said, my voice cracking with emotion as my tiny mother sat up in bed and reached out to touch Neng Yao and strained to see him with eyes that had grown very dim.

"Is this really my son? Is this really my baby?"

"Yes, mama, this is your son. This is your baby."

He stood still while she felt of him all over, her lined face luminous with joy. I could see it was hard for her to believe he had grown up to be such a man. I knew too she must have been thinking about how good God had been to her, to let her live to know her prayers were answered and that her son was in a free land where he could come to know Jesus. I sensed with a great sadness—but peace, too—that her work on earth was finished now, and she was free to go to be with the Lord.

Later that day, Neng Yao took the heart of a fresh-cut watermelon to mama in her room, and sat with her while she ate it. There were very few words between them, because words were not needed. But heart was speaking to heart, and it was good.

A week later, I told Neng Yao and his dear wife how God had miraculously raised our mother from death in April of 1977, and how she had prayed faithfully for his release for many years. I told them how God had moved to secure their freedom, and that He loved them enough to send His only Son Jesus to die for them and enable them to become sons of God.

How eagerly they listened. And miraculously, in spite of all the brainwashing to which he had been subjected in Communist China, Neng Yao had kept freedom in his heart and had known, somehow, there was a real God somewhere and he would find Him someday. Right away, he realized that Jesus was the One, and that this was the day of salvation for them all. In a moment, Neng Yao and his wife were on their knees, confessing their sins and asking Jesus to come live in their hearts. When I gave Chinese Bibles to my brother and his wife, I wept as I watched the eagerness with which they pored over the pages of the Word of life.

Neng Yao soon found an excellent job in a chemical lab near San Jose, and before long they were moving from the house in our backyard to a place of their own. Little Mike was happy in preschool, making new American friends, and my brother and his wife were learning to drive, to speak and understand English, and to live as free people.

I cannot say that the hours I spent with my brother "catching up" on twenty years of news were pure joy. Many times I was reduced to tears by the things he shared about our beloved homeland, reflecting the same reality Colonel Fan had told me about earlier in the year.

But one of the personal, family things Neng Yao shared with me brought a different reaction.

One day the Communists had contacted him, and said they needed the land on which our father had been buried after his murder in 1958. They exhumed his body and called my brother to come to identify it. Later, they had cremated him and given his ashes to Neng Yao, so now the ashes were in the United States, awaiting our disposition of them.

While Neng Yao was telling me the details of these things, it suddenly dawned on me that God's promise was completely fulfilled:

Our whole family had gotten out of Red China!

27

MERRY CHRISTMAS

On November 6, God told me to begin a time of fasting and prayer again.

"Why, Lord?"

"Don't ask why, just do it."

"But Lord, Thanksgiving is coming, a time of celebration. And You have given me so much to celebrate this year. You know that I like to eat as much as anybody. Is fasting and prayer Your only answer for everything? Why do You always make me do it, when some people have never heard of it?"

He didn't explain, so I began to fast.

On Thanksgiving Day, S. K., Neng Yao, and I went to Virginia Beach to be with Pat Robertson and his wife Dede. Everyone else was enjoying the feast of turkey and all that goes with it, but I was just sitting there looking at my empty plate.

"What's on your heart during this fast, Nora?" Pat asked.

"I don't know what's on my heart, Pat, but it sure is heavy, like a burden burning inside me."

"How long is the fast going to last?"

"I don't know that either. The Lord didn't tell me." But I was about to find out.

On December 15, around six o'clock in the afternoon, the Chinese consul in San Francisco called me with terrible news:

"In just a little while it will be announced that President Carter is cancelling the United States defense treaty with Taiwan. He is going to "normalize" relations with Red China and officially recognize the Peking Communist dictatorship as the legitimate government."

How could he? I was shocked with horror, grieved beyond words that a born-again President could cancel a treaty to please a government that had brutally murdered ninety million Chinese people.

My heart was so broken that I couldn't go to bed and sleep that night. I closed myself in the bathroom, where I wouldn't be disturbing the rest of the family, and fell on my face before the Lord.

"Oh, Jesus!" I cried, "help the precious people on Taiwan to keep their freedom, to save their lives. Don't let them fall before the awful Communist slavery."

I remembered how the Communists had tortured me, murdered my father, and butchered millions of innocent people who hadn't done anything wrong. I thought about all the terrible conditions my brother had told me about in Red China—no freedom of speech, no freedom of press, no freedom of movement, no freedom to own a Bible and worship God. No freedom to keep what you have earned. No freedom to decide for yourself where to live, what to do. No freedom to vote and elect leaders of your choice. No freedom to speak against tyranny without the threat of imprisonment or death. People starving, little children, the sick and the aged being forced to work many grueling hours a day and then being sent off to be killed when their bodies were worn out and they were no longer useful to the State. No freedom to live . . .

"Oh, God, don't let that happen to Taiwan!"

I thought of the thousands of people who had received

the Lord at our Crusades, and how their lives might soon be in danger if they dared to speak of their faith. How I longed to be with them, to comfort them, to give them encouragement, to hold their hand. My heart was bleeding for them.

"Lord, what can I do? What can I do to help my people?"

It was almost morning when He spoke to me in an audible voice:

"Read Jeremiah 26."

I sat up on the cold white tile floor, leaned my back against the wall, and opened my Bible. The scripture was so plain—telling me not to leave out one word of all God wanted the people on Taiwan to hear. I was to tell them the whole truth, and maybe then they would turn from idol worship and begin to worship the true and living God. If they would obey His laws and listen to His servants, He would preserve them. He would not let them be destroyed.

"Go to them now," He said.

It was almost Christmas. The tree was ready, and the children were so excited—Paul and his wife Susie, Ruthie, Joe and his wife Sue, and the four little orphans I'd adopted from overseas. Gloria was five, Wei-Wei was three, and the twins, Julie and Jackie, were only fifteen months old. I'd already been on the road over two hundred days out of the last year. And I knew it would probably be the last Christmas my precious seventy-six-year-old mother would have with us on earth. It would be the first Christmas in America for Neng Yao and his family . . .

It would be terribly hard to leave them all at such a time, a real sacrifice.

"Christmas means Jesus, and Jesus means sacrifice," the Lord reminded me. "I've had you on a fast for forty days and forty nights to prepare you to be My soldier and go tell Taiwan about Me while their hearts are newly broken and they are ready to hear. If they will turn to Me, I can save their land."

Then He told me something else.

"Remember, My daughter, if you wait for perfect conditions, you will never get anything done."

"Yes, Lord."

When I announced to the family that I was leaving for Taiwan right away, everybody was in an uproar:

"Mom! You can't mean that you're going to go now, with Christmas coming up so soon!"

"Christmas is nothing if I don't serve Jesus," I said. "If ever I needed to go, I need to go now. God has told me the hearts of the people are open to hear. Ruthie, I want you to go with me. And S. K., I need you to stay home with the family."

When I called Mr. Lee Shih-feng at the Broadcasting Corporation of China to tell him I would soon be on my way over, he tried to talk me out of it too.

"Please don't come. Things are very uncertain here right now."

Uncertain or not, I could see it was an important hour for me to visit Taiwan. The people thought they had lost a friend in President Carter, but I could tell them they had gained a million friends among Christians who were going to be faithful to keep on praying for them, and to send Bibles to them.

When I left for the airport, S. K. and the big kids knew I had to obey the Lord, but Wei-Wei cried and held onto my hand.

"Mama, when will you come back?" My heart was too full to answer. My family cried, and I cried too, all the way across the ocean. Our plane was almost empty as it droned the many hours through the skies to Taiwan. When Ruth and I landed in Taipei on December 23, the airport was almost empty too. Planes had been canceled.

Nobody wanted to go in or out of Taiwan, because they were afraid there might be riots. They didn't know what was going to happen. I didn't know what was going to happen either, but I knew that God was in charge.

When we got off the airplane, I had no itinerary, nothing planned. It had been like that when I had landed on the island nearly ten years ago—there was no meeting scheduled until God opened one little church and performed signs and wonders when I lifted up His name to a tiny congregation. Would He do something like that again?

Mr. Lee Shih-feng met us at the airport and took us to the President Hotel. Riding through the streets, I saw the whole city was like death. Everyone looked frightened and worried, as if their hearts were broken. I wanted to roll down the windows and shout at them, "Beloved, your security wasn't in America! Your security is in Jesus!" But they wouldn't have understood.

Everywhere I went on the island, the press received me with open arms. They had so many questions to ask me, and I had so many answers to give them. God arranged for me to be on television morning, noon, and night every day, and the whole island was watching and listening.

"Why did you come at this hour?"

"I came because Jesus has a message for you," I said. Then I opened the Bible to 2 Chronicles 7:14, read it, and explained that if they would humble themselves and pray and turn from their wicked ways of idol worship to worship the true and living God, He would hear from heaven, save His people, and heal their land.

"If you really love your country," I said, "you have to become God's people so He can bless your land." I told them to write our office in Taipei, and we would send them a Bible that would tell them more about this God who is real.

Everywhere I went after the television broadcasts, I told

199

the people that their security wasn't in American soldiers and their weapons, but in the Lord Jesus Christ. And that although the American soldiers who had been protecting them were going to leave them, Jesus would be with them always.

God had told me not to leave out a word, and I didn't.

On Christmas eve, the fact that Ruth and I were thousands of miles from our family suddenly hit me. As the old spirit of loneliness began to engulf me, the Holy Spirit reminded me of the children at the Bethany Children's Home in Taipei, the orphanage with the swimming pool.

I might not be able to spend Christmas day with my own husband and family, but I could spend it with more than a hundred children who had no families of their own. Johnson Han, my wonderful friend who had been director of the orphanage for many years, had gone to be with the Lord just before Thanksgiving. It would be the children's first Christmas without their beloved "Papa."

Actually, he had been old enough to be their grandfather, but none of the children had seemed to notice that his hair was white and his step was slow. He was the one who knew each of them by name and loved them as his own. Besides being their papa, Johnson Han was their pastor, their teacher, their counselor, and their friend. The children had learned to relate to their heavenly Father through the life and example of Johnson Han. They would be brokenhearted without him.

The children had already suffered so much—the loss of their own parents, the loneliness and rejection and stigma of being orphans. Most of them had also suffered poverty and the lack of enough food and clothing, and now they were suffering again.

I knew how they must feel. If I could, I would scoop them all up in my arms and tell them I love them and take them all home to live with me. But that wasn't possible.

There was something I *could* do, though, and Ruth and I began to do it.

We arrived at the home the next morning with our arms loaded down with brightly wrapped presents. The children ran out to greet us, their hearts and eyes overflowing with joy that they had not been forgotten on Christmas day.

As we gathered together in the little chapel, I told the children that God loved them enough to send His very own Son to be their Savior, so they could live together with Him. And He loved them enough to bring me all the way from America to spend Christmas day with them.

When I had finished talking, several children who had not already given their lives to the Lord invited Him into their hearts. It made my Christmas joy complete.

And the day after Christmas, the Lord had another surprise in store for us. On that day, the Lord told me to go to Quemoy Island, just three miles from Mainland China, and to take a lot of Bibles with me. My heart leaped for joy!

Just a year earlier, I had learned that the government of the Republic of China had developed highly accurate radio-controlled balloons which could be directed into every part of Mainland China, carrying up to four hundred pounds of cargo each. They had been successfully using the balloons for many years to drop food, medicine, clothing, and anti-Communist literature on the Mainland. And when I had heard reports of the success of this project and seen actual pictures and letters received by the government confirming its effectiveness, I had immediately begun to think of its great potential for spreading the gospel. I had prayed and prayed, and now, a year later, God was bringing about the miracle.

Normally, government balloons were used only for government purposes. But because I had gone to Taiwan in her hour of need, and because they knew of my desire to fight Communism with the Word of God, the government leaders were glad to give me special clearance to go to Quemoy, and even to take me there.

It was a cold rainy day, and I was soaking wet when I toured the island where many things, such as hospitals, are built underground. I saw soldiers come out on the field to blow up the balloons ten stories high. And when I asked permission to send Bibles in one of them, they said, "Of course we will let you send Bibles—as many as you want."

With my own hands, I helped put the Bibles into waterproof packages and place them in the balloon. Then I personally launched our first load of Bibles into Mainland China. It was a dream come true.

As I watched the balloons rise majestically into the sky and soar high above the water until they were out of sight over the Mainland, I felt my heart was in the balloon with the Bibles. And the Lord reminded me of the scripture in which He promises that His Word will not return void, but will accomplish that for which He sends it. To me, that meant that Red China would have a great revival someday, because every part of that country would have the gospel in its hands, and nothing would be able to stop that revival, not even the gates of hell.

28

THE BOAT PEOPLE

Before Ruth and I had left the United States for Taiwan, a member of the congregation at Melodyland Christian Center sent me a clipping from the *Los Angeles Times* about 134 boat people who had escaped from Communist-dominated lands—and about the thirty-four who had survived the awful voyage.

"I think you should try to see these people while you're overseas," he wrote.

"Oh, that man has such a big heart," I said to myself. "He's always got something going." I thought he was crazy to think I could find the thirty-four boat people and talk to them. I wouldn't have any idea where to find them.

But God knew where they were, and where He was going to send me.

The day Ruth and I went to Kaohsiung, the thirty-four survivors were arriving at the refugee camp on Makung Island, only an hour's flying time away. We took a load of Chinese Bibles and went to the camp on December 27.

Thousands of emaciated refugees were there—a heartbreaking sight. Thin, ragged, their skin burned by sun and sea, their hollow eyes filled with pain and grief, they jammed the rows of low barracks overflowing with bunk beds and tables crowded together for mealtime.

Some of the boat people were from Vietnam, some from Cambodia, some from Communist China and other places. All had one thing in common—they had preferred the uncertain future of venturing into the open sea in rickety fishing boats or makeshift rafts with only meager supplies to staying in their Communist-dominated homelands.

God arranged for Wang Yeong-Gen, the young captain of the boat on which thirty-four people made it to freedom, to come out and tell me his horrendous story. His family—eleven in all, including his grandmother and other relatives—had decided in the spring to attempt an escape from the Communist oppression in Vietnam. Although they knew they might be captured or lost at sea, they decided to make the attempt.

"Why did you want to escape when you knew it would be so dangerous?" I asked the young captain as he began to tell me his story.

For answer, he shrugged his shoulders and asked *me* a question:

"Without freedom, what is the use of living?" That was how all of them had felt, and I understood the feeling.

Yeong-Gen and several friends had pooled their meager savings and purchased a boat three yards wide and fifteen yards long. To learn the treacherous water routes to the open sea, they had filled the boat with wood twice a month and pretended to be selling it while they practiced for their escape. October 1 was set as the date.

On September 30, they sent the old people and children ahead in a tiny fishing boat, planning to pick them up later. Such a feeble crew would not arouse any suspicion. The next day, the rest of them loaded their boat and began their journey out of Saigon Harbor about seven o'clock in the morning. They were dressed in Communist clothing and appeared to be on another innocent wood-selling expedition.

The first day passed without incident. Then, at three o'clock on the morning of October 2, when they had been at sea for twenty hours, suddenly a Communist police boat came into view and started observing them. The boat people began to sing Communist songs as enthusiastically as they could, and pretended to be fishing. After several minutes—which seemed like hours—the police allowed them to pass.

A few hours later, they rendezvoused with the small boatload of elderly people and children, and helped them climb aboard the larger vessel. Now their total number was forty-five—the number for which they had adequate food and other provisions to sustain them until they reached a free land.

But later that day and in the days that followed, they came upon other smaller, less-seaworthy boats filled with desperate refugees who begged to be taken on board. They could not turn anyone away, and within a few days they had three times as many people on board as they had planned for.

There were moments when other Communist police boats came into view, but miraculously the refugees were not seen. Their original plan had been to sail to Malaysia, but with so many people on board there was no chance of making it that far. So they changed their destination to the Philippines. On the fourth day their engine died, and they had to depend on the wind and makeshift sails. On the eighth day, a huge storm arose, and they were driven by the wind and the rain to a small island, but were unable to land because of the severity of the storm. Almost all their few possessions were swept away by the towering waves which came crashing down into the boat, and many died. But that was only the beginning of their sorrows.

The next forty-two days were one continuous nightmare. Supplies of food and water were quickly exhausted.

The little rainwater they had managed to catch for drinking purposes was gone, and everyone started to become dehydrated. The babies cried for food and water, but there was none to give them. When they could stand their thirst no longer, some of them drank their own urine. Others gulped the salty sea water and began to hemorrhage and die.

On October 18, Yeong-Gen's two-year-old baby breathed his last. The baby's eyes were so dry from dehydration that the little lids could not be shut. Lovingly, the parents wrapped the little body in a shirt and dropped it into the sea. A few days later, their three-year-old died, and then the four-year-old. By November 2, all four of their children were gone. Yeong-Gen and his wife had no more tears to cry. In all, seven members of their own family died, and there was still no hope in sight.

"I didn't know it at the time," Yeong-Gen said, "but there was an eighty-seven-year-old woman on board who had been praying to her God every day. She did it silently, because she knew none of the rest of us shared her faith, but she was asking her God to send a ship to take us out. She believed He would do it for her."

One day they sighted a large Japanese ship and begged to be allowed on board, but their request was denied. Then there was a Korean ship, one from Malaysia, and later a British ship, and a few others. But none would give them food or water. All left them alone to die. Finally, on November 18, they spotted a ship from Taiwan whose crew spoke their language! The next day they were permitted to board, but some were too far gone to be revived.

By the time the ship reached Taiwan, only thirty-four of the original boat people remained alive. All were in such critical condition that they were hospitalized for twenty days. They had just been released to be brought to the refugee camp.

I could not stop my tears as Yeong-Gen related his story. I felt such a surge of God's love for them! When one of the refugees asked me, "Why did you come to see us now? Isn't it a big holiday in your country? Aren't people celebrating something there? Why aren't you at home?" I cried, "Oh, let me tell you about Jesus!"

The captain and his wife gathered the thirty-four surviving refugees from their boat together, and I told them about the Son of God who chose to die that they might live forever. Every single one of them bowed his head and invited Jesus into his life. I gave them the Bibles I had brought with me, and they began to read with great interest and spiritual hunger. How grateful I was to God for sending me.

I was thankful, too, that I had shared their suffering. That I had known what it was to be hungry and thirsty, and how it felt to see a loved one die. And I was thankful most of all that I was ready to tell them the reason for the hope that was in me, so they could have the Hope of the world for themselves.

29

RETURN TRIP

On January 22, the Lord told me to go back to Taiwan again.

"But Lord, I just got home! I haven't rested yet!"

"There is no time for you to rest."

I jumped on the plane and went back to Taiwan. The Taiwan news TV followed me wherever I went, encouraging everyone from the heads of the government all the way down to the peasants in the rice paddies not to be discouraged. I told people about our upcoming July Crusade and their need to turn from worshiping idols to worshiping the living God so He can bless their country.

We even paid a visit to the refugee camp again. Once more someone asked me why I wanted to come.

"Once I was a refugee just like you are," I told them. "God helped me escape from Red China because I had accepted Jesus Christ as my Lord. The same Jesus is still on the throne and I have a duty to tell others about Him."

Hundreds listened this time, as I told them about who Jesus is and how they could have the same Lord. Many had already been reading the Bibles I had left there on my previous visit, and many refugees knelt down on the bunks, beside the bunks, and on the rocky shore outside to receive the Lord. For them, the long journey was over. They had finally found rest and peace in the arms of Jesus.

"Whom the Lord sets free is free indeed," I told them.

On February 15, the Lord told me to make my third trip to Taiwan since normalization, and I thought I would go out of my mind.

"How can a person go on like this?" I asked Him.

But even while I complained, I knew that while the day is here, we have to work. When night comes, it will be too late. And when I thought I had no strength for the task, God made His strength perfect in my weakness.

This third trip after normalization was the hardest of all. I was sick on the road, but God opened up a wonderful new opportunity for me that made it all worthwhile.

I didn't know when I was planning my February itinerary that I would be arriving in Kaohsiung, the large southern seaport city, on the day of one of the country's largest patriotic "love country" rallies. Over one hundred thousand people were expected to attend, and speakers were coming from many nations to address the crowd.

Just before my departure from the United States, I received a telephone call from one of the government officials in Kaohsiung, inviting me to be an honored guest at the rally.

Immediately I knew in my spirit that the Lord had something special in store. The Holy Spirit prompted me to call the Mayor of Kaohsiung and ask his permission to distribute Bibles at the rally.

Mayor Wang Yu-yun, although he was a Buddhist and had not yet made a personal commitment to the Lord, had attended our 1977 Crusade and had listened to the sermons with tears rolling down his cheeks. And he had helped pass out the Word of God to the thousands who had streamed forward for salvation. He had seen first-hand how eager they were to receive the Bibles, and so he graciously granted me permission to distribute Bibles at the rally, of which he was one of the sponsors.

Immediately I cabled my Taiwan secretary, instructing her to have the ministry's entire stock of Chinese Bibles taken to the rally site. Before the rally day was ended, all seventy thousand of them had been handed out to men, women, and children, most of them from idol-worshiping backgrounds. I knew the Word would do its work, and I was freshly impressed that God's methods and His timing are always perfect.

Months later, I had to remind myself of that. On June 24, 1979, at 12:55 P.M., just two weeks before I was to leave America for the Crusade, the Lord called my beloved mother home to be with Him.

What anguish tore at my heart! What feelings of loss overwhelmed me! Yet underneath my human emotions was a deep peace that she was released from her suffer-ings and resting in the everlasting arms of Jesus. When I thought that in my grief I couldn't go to Taiwan to preach, the Lord told me there were millions of mothers there who might never know Him unless I went to tell them about Him. Then there was no way I could keep from going. I realized again that God can use for His glory *whatever* comes into our lives, if it makes us more His instruments to tell the world of His great love.

The Crusade that was born in the heartbreak of normal-ization of relations with Red China, the tragedy of the boat people, and the sorrow of my mother's passing yielded a rich harvest for the Kingdom of our God.

30

BACK TO THE MAINLAND

As soon as the July Crusade was over in Kaohsiung, there were big meetings in the Philippines, with an opportunity to pray for thousands who wanted a healing touch from the Lord. Then I was on the road again in the United States, speaking in churches all over the country to raise funds for Bibles and more Bibles to spread the Word of God in the Far East, where a billion people are in desperate need of it.

No wonder I was tired, no wonder I wanted to stay at home and rest for a while, but there was no rest.

On August 19, I was sitting before a congregation in Spokane, Washington, when the Lord gave me one of the most startling pronouncements of my life:

"It is time for you to go to Mainland China."

At first I was shocked. All the terrors of all I had suffered under the Communists flooded my mind, and I couldn't *believe* He would want me to return to the land from which I had barely escaped with my life.

But His sheep can hear His voice and recognize it. I could not pretend to be deaf. I walked to the pulpit, grabbed its sides for support, and with tears streaming down I said, "My heavenly Father has just told me to return to my homeland."

I heard some people gasp with surprise, just as I had done. Then, without thinking any further about what I could hardly comprehend, I preached. When I had finished praying for people afterward, I called home and told S. K. and the kids. After they recovered from their surprise, they said they would get the ball rolling for a new passport, the necessary visa, and the rest of the details.

As soon as the meetings in Spokane were over, I went home to make my own preparations. But after twenty-one years, what contacts could I make? How could I ever find anybody? When and with whom could I travel?

In the natural, everything was as impossible as usual. And as usual, while we took care of the things that were possible, the Lord moved the mountains and accomplished the impossible. It took several miracles for all the details to be worked out, but I was used to miracles by now. Almost the next thing I knew, I was in the San Francisco airport with my friend Mrs. Ralph Wilkerson, boarding a plane bound for Tokyo. There we would join a group of American tourists which included our attorney friend, Herb Ellingwood, for a ten-day visit to Mainland China. S. K. would take my place and speak at meetings that had been scheduled for months, and he would come to the Mainland on another trip two weeks later with Pat Robertson.

By overseas telephone, I had been able to contact my old girlfriend, Nancy, in Shanghai, and she had promised to meet me in Peking to help me contact the underground church.

During the long hours on the plane, I had time to pray and sort out my thoughts. I had to admit that some of them were full of fear because of all I had suffered at the hands of the Communists. Now I was voluntarily going back into their territory.

In Tokyo, all members of the tour group were given an

intensive briefing. We were warned to "behave as Christians," giving offense to no one, but we were not to indicate in any other way that we had any official Christian connection. If we did, we would be jeopardizing the possibility of entry of other groups to the Mainland in the future. We were told it was safe enough for us to take a few Bibles into the Mainland if we could fit them into the one small suitcase we would be permitted to carry, but we were not to offer Bibles or other Christian literature to our guides or to people on the street. We could expect to be kept busy from early morning until late at night, so there would be little opportunity for us to "get into trouble."

Late Sunday afternoon, October 28, we flew from Tokyo to Peking (now Beijing), the capital of Communist China, the city where I had been born forty-seven years ago. When our plane touched down at the airport and I saw a Communist soldier for the first time in more than twenty years, I thought my heart was going to stop. I could almost hear the interminable screaming questions again, smell the backbreaking loads of coal under the burning sun, suffer the thirst, the hunger, the kicks against my baby-swollen middle, see the blood-drenched sheets of my father's deathbed, hear the whine of bullets . . .

My tortured imaginings were mercifully brought to a sudden halt by the loud question of the man at the customs and immigration desk. I was shocked back to 1979 again. It was midnight, and I was the last of our tour group to go through the line.

"Have you any friends or relatives in China?" The question was asked me in Chinese, but I pretended not to understand. The official asked me again, louder, as if he knew I *could* understand, but finally, when I did not reply, he gave up and asked his questions in English.

"Have you any relatives or friends in China?"

"I don't have any immediate family here," I shrugged, trying to sound as if it didn't matter. I didn't dare let him know I had already been in touch with Nancy on the overseas telephone before I left America. I was afraid it wouldn't be safe for her.

Next he wanted to know what I was doing in China.

I answered with a nonchalant, "Visiting as a tourist," and after a few more questions, to which I gave the briefest possible answers, he let me through.

Immediately upon our arrival at our hotel, Herb Ellingwood and another American friend and I took a taxi to try to find Nancy. When I had talked with her on the phone from California and asked her to meet me in Peking, I'd had no idea at which hotel I'd be staying or what time I'd arrive, so she had given me some directions to the place where she'd be waiting for me.

After two hours of driving through back alleys and looking in all the wrong places, we finally found the address where she was staying. It was so late that the household had gone to sleep, and we had to pound on the door to waken her. When she finally came to the door, she was wearing a robe over her pajamas and had her hair done up in curlers. She literally screamed when she saw me, and pinched my arms to see if I was real.

Oh, she had so much to tell me. We talked and listened and prayed and cried far into the night. And, in a few short days, I had enough amazing encounters to fill a book—finding old friends who had kept the faith, hearing about others who had died for theirs, reliving a lifetime in Peking, Shanghai, and Canton as I visited places and people who had been meaningful in my life:

The grimy, tile-roofed hospital where I had entered the world, learning that my "real mother" had later married and had babies she could keep to love. Running my hands over the peeling paint on the walls of the school at Shanghai, seeing the dark stucco shambles of grandmother's house that had been turned into a factory, its old fishpond that had once mirrored the moon became a parking lot for bicycles, the sides of the street that had once held carefully trimmed shrubbery now littered with rubbish. Meeting a cousin I hadn't seen for twenty-one years and leading him and his family to Jesus. Weeping at seeing a young man whose father had "written him" a Bible from verses he had memorized before the mandatory burning of Bibles in the "cultural revolution." Seeing the awful poverty of the people in drab clothing, just as my brother had described them to me. Attending the powerless "worship services" staged for the benefit of tourists in Shanghai and Canton, one or two churches open in each city of millions of people. Learning of inadequate wages, looking at buildings in bad repair. Meeting Christians who would give anything for a Bible . . .

Of all that I saw and experienced in those days, two sharply contrasted pictures stand out in my mind:

One, a ragged, blue clad, toothless old woman, her gray black hair hanging in long braids, struggling to push a falling-apart wheelbarrow of green vegetables along a bumpy street, her humped shoulders eloquent of age and pain, her eyes dull with the hopeless dogged endurance of a person without the Lord.

The other, what happened one night when several believers gathered for an evening meal in my girlfriend's second-floor apartment in Shanghai. She had a piano in her bedroom, and after we had eaten, Mrs. Wilkerson sat down to play the piano so we could sing together. We sang softly at first, so no one outside could hear and report us. There were still songs we all knew and could sing together: "O Come All Ye Faithful" and "Silent Night, Holy Night."

As we sang, something seemed to happen inside us all.

The words brought courage to our hearts, strength to our voices, joy to our spirits that couldn't be quenched. Soon we were singing loudly, enthusiastically, as if we had forgotten how important it was to be quiet because someone might be listening.

Or maybe we hadn't forgotten anything. Maybe we were suddenly remembering something: "Greater is He that is in me, than He that is in the world." Maybe gathered together in the name of Jesus we were experiencing His presence, according to His promise. Maybe with the Word of God in their hands, new Bibles we had taken to them, the Chinese Christians knew the Perfect Love that casts out all fear, and they were so certain at that moment that He was with them that they would never be afraid again. Ever.

Maybe? No, not maybe. For certain. Because right then God confirmed His Word through the mouth of one of the Chinese women, sister to my best girlfriend in high school. The woman's name was Lulu, and she spoke to us all:

"Nora Lam Sung, before you came and brought us the Word of God, I wanted with all my heart to get out of Red China, to leave this land where I've suffered so much and never to return again." She opened her new Bible and pressed it close to her heart before she went on, blinking back tears of new commitment and joy: "But now, I want to stay forever and help my people to know the living God."

31

CHINA CRY

"How do you feel about Mainland China today and the Communists there?" someone asked me recently.

I answered that I just want to love the people and tell them about Jesus. I cannot deny that the Communists took away our freedom, that they tortured me, murdered my father, and butchered millions of my people. But I can't limit God's love. God's love is for everyone.

The door to Mainland China is cracked open now, but perhaps only for a season. We can go in, but we must act quickly. Time is limited. He is coming soon. And the way has been prepared.

One day God showed me how He used even godless Mao Tse Tung to pave the way for the coming of Jesus into the hearts of the Chinese people:

Mao got rid of idol worship in Mainland China by making it illegal. God used Mao to make one language—Mandarin—mandatory for the whole country, thus facilitating the spread of the gospel. And then Mao, who had tried to make himself God to the people, met the fate of all mortal men. He died, leaving a big vacuum in the hearts of the people, a vacuum that only the living God can fill.

With all these things in mind, I realize the awesome urgency of the hour. And recently God showed me three

217

major thrusts that are imperative for our programs right now if we are to be His instruments:

1) Radio. Through radio it is now possible to proclaim the Gospel to all of Mainland China. We have been effectively using radio since 1973 to beam God's Word every day to Taiwan and to much of the Chinese Mainland. Our new goal must be to search out new, more powerful transmitting stations that can carry the message of salvation to every corner of China—a land with a population five times that of the United States. The same radio broadcasts can also be syndicated to major Chinese population centers through the free world.

2) Bible distribution. The greatest single need of the Chinese people is the Word of God, the "Bread of Life." God has given us the unique opportunity of distributing hundreds of thousands of Chinese Bibles throughout Mainland China by radio-controlled balloons launched from Quemoy. We must not let this tremendous opportunity slip through our fingers. Immediate distribution of hundreds of thousands of copies of God's Word is a key priority.

3) Television. Another important goal God has laid on my heart is using the medium of television to reach the forty-two million free Chinese around the world with the gospel. They know the languages and culture behind the Bamboo Curtain, and many of them still have friends and relatives there. They also have the finances and the mobility to evangelize the Mainland. And while Chinese people are often distrustful of Westerners, they are open and receptive to other Chinese.

Time is running short. The destiny of millions of souls is hanging in the balance. What we do in the remaining time before Christ's return will determine where millions of Chinese souls will spend eternity.

Recently I reread a letter that God's prophet Jim Gerrard had written to S. K. and to me in 1973, two years after he had prophesied that God would use me in the Far East. In the letter written to both of us, he said:

God has opened the door in Taiwan for you! The "white" missionaries do not have this "special favor" that God has created with you two. You are the ones He will use. Believe it. Accept it.

God has told me He is opening a huge door involving the salvation of Chinese. And He says, "When I open that Door, no man can shut it." There is coming a Holy Ghost bonfire sweep of souls into the Kingdom. It will spread like a prairie fire. People who do not see it will just not believe it. But you two shall see it, and believe it . . . for you fit into God's great plans.

God spoke to my heart, "As it happened in Indonesia, so it will happen in China. Nothing is too hard for Me. When the time comes, who will prevent Me? Will walls, or laws, or armies, or guns?" And I saw that no man can build up walls high enough to stop the winds, and the Spirit of God moves in like the winds . . . and what man is able to resist what God will do by His Spirit?

All the so-called power of the Communist rulers on the mainland of China was as nothing compared to what God could do. God sits in His heaven and laughs at the puny insolence of men. The Communists pass laws saying you cannot worship God. They persecute the people. They burn the Bibles—which contain the Word of God! And God sees it all. He knows. He is aware of the suffering and tears of His people. . . .

God tolerates a thing just so long. And then He begins to prepare a man . . . or a woman . . . or a few men . . . to serve Him. They are men and women who dedicate themselves. They are Spirit-led servants. They are not afraid to go out against the enemy. God has given them "tokens" of His Almighty power.

God does not need to wait for an "open door." He *creates* history. He alone opens doors.

God has a people in China. He always keeps a remnant. And He has heard the cries of His people. He has seen their afflictions. He has remembered His covenant. He is faithful. And He will move in ways of great wonders to save these people.

There is a great explosion of God's power coming to these oppressed countries very soon. . . . He will bring a deliverance that will stagger the imaginations of men. He is not going to tolerate the name of His Covenant-Bearer Jesus to suffer the shame and degradation of ungodly oppressors much longer. He will keep His covenant.

God showed me how easy it was to take a nation like Indonesia, and to deliver her from Communistic oppression. It was done by signs, miracles, and wonders. And God allowed me to know that He was going to do a work in China thought impossible by people of little or no faith. He told me plainly that He was going to do an Indonesian-type work in all of China. . . .

Nora and S. K., I know that God has called you two! You are to be part of the great deliverance for China. God has already given you "tokens of His power." You know that if He sends you, He will be with you. . . .

That was what Jim Gerrard had written, and that is what would be done, because a true prophet of God had spoken it. It would have to come true.

And one day a few years ago, when I had been very discouraged about my ministry, having forgotten the prophecies, I received an exciting phone call from Sue Westbrook, another American friend through whom God had spoken His will to me in 1972. Sue had such tremendous news she couldn't wait to tell me all about it:

A teacher in a Christian school in California was taking a night class at Stanford University. She was seated beside a man from Mainland China, learned he was a Christian, and asked him for his testimony.

He gave it to her straightforwardly, without embellishment:

"I was a sharpshooter in Communist China, assigned to a firing squad. One day a woman was brought before us who admitted to being a Christian. She wouldn't deny her God, but prayed aloud to Him during the last three minutes she had to live. We tried three times to shoot her, but each time we heard the count to fire a brilliant light came down from the sky, blinding us. Our guns became almost too hot to hold, and as we squeezed the triggers the guns were jerked upward by some unseen force. This happened three times.

"I knew that if I was unable to kill this woman, I would be killed myself, so I dropped my gun and ran. Miraculously, no one pursued me, and I escaped and found my way to a Catholic convent. The Sisters took me in. I told them I knew there was a God, and that I had been taught wrongly by the Communists, for I had seen Him at work when one of His followers called on His name.

"I wanted to know the kind of God that woman knew, that real God with real power. There in the convent I met Jesus."

When Sue had finished relaying the testimony to me, I fell on my knees.

"Oh, dear Jesus," I cried, remembering the inner prompting on that fateful day to call on the name of my Lord aloud and ask Him to let me and my son live. "Oh, dear Jesus, forgive me for being discouraged. Thank You for letting me know that the first time I ever lifted up Your name, You won a lost soul to Yourself. Lord, don't ever let me be discouraged again. Keep me reminded that I have only to lift up the blessed name of Jesus, and You will do the rest—You will draw all men unto You. Amen."

I was thinking about that testimony and about Jim Gerrard's prophecy as I looked out the window of the train before our departure from Canton for Hong Kong and then back to America. Suddenly I saw a Communist soldier standing at the edge of the platform. This time, my heart didn't almost stop. It beat faster. The fear was gone! Instead of seeing him as my enemy, I knew he was someone for whom Jesus had died, and I believed that God had brought me out of Red China twenty-one years ago so I could learn His Word and someday go back and win that soldier for Jesus. How I need your prayers and support!

By the time the train started to move slowly out of the station, my faith had soared to believe that one day God would let me go back to hold a Crusade in Mainland China, where He will save thousands upon thousands upon thousands.

Too much to ask, you think? Too much to expect, even of God Almighty? Oh, no, beloved. Nothing is too hard for our God.

My brothers and sisters, I am not afraid. I hear the cry of China for God. Do you hear it too?

Will you go with me to lift up the name of Jesus—that at the name of Jesus, every knee shall bow, and every tongue confess that Jesus Christ is Lord?

If we will do our little part, God will do His big part.

I know.

For more information about the ministry of Nora Lam Sung, or to schedule her for a meeting in your area, write or phone:

**Nora Lam Ministries
P.O. Box 24466
San Jose, California 95154
Telephone (408) 267-5451**

All contributions are tax deductible.